Chip Wood

# YARDSTICKS

## Children in the Classroom Ages 4–14

*A Resource for Parents and Teachers*

NORTHEAST FOUNDATION FOR CHILDREN

All net proceeds from the sale of *Yardsticks: Children in the Classroom Ages 4–14; A Resource for Parents and Teachers* support the work of Northeast Foundation for Children, Inc. NEFC is a nonprofit, educational foundation established to demonstrate through teaching, research, and consultation, a sensible and systematic approach to schooling.

ISBN 0-9618636-4-1

Library of Congress catalog card number 96-070570

Expanded Edition: Second Printing June 1997

Northeast Foundation for Children, Inc.
71 Montague City Rd.
Greenfield, MA 01301
1-800-360-6332

Excerpt from *Black Children: Social, Educational, and Parental Environments* by Harriette Pipes McAdoo and John Lewis McAdoo (Beverly Hills, CA: Sage Publications, 1985) used by permission.

Excerpt from *First Grade Takes a Test* by Miriam Cohen (William Morrow & Co., Inc.: New York, NY, 1980) used by permission.

Chart material for ages 5–7 was originally adapted from Frances Ilg, *Scoring Notes: The Developmental Examination* (New Haven, CT: 1965) and has since been modified through further reading, research and observation. Other original source material supporting the charts is found in the bibliography.

Interior design by Gian Lombardo, Quale Press

Cover design by Rebecca Neimark, 26 Letters

For Reenie

*In tribute to Dr. Louise Bates Ames (1908–1996)
for her life-long contributions to the well-being of children.
Dr. Ames, colleague of Dr. Arnold Gesell and co-founder
of Gesell Institute of Child Development,
devoted her career to help parents and teachers
better understand their children.*

# Contents

*Each contains: narrative description, growth patterns,
classroom implications, appropriate curriculum*

*"How old would you be if you didn't know how old you were?"*

Attributed to Satchel Paige

♦

*"In order to be treated fairly and equally, children have to be treated differently."*

Melvin Konner, *Childhood: A Multicultural View*

# Preface to the Expanded Edition

This book is about children in school. It is designed for both parents and teachers and provides easy reference to expectations about children's growth and development in the classroom, now for ages 4-14.

I have tried in this small volume to consolidate a good deal of theory with years of professional experience in schools. My goal continues to be to present important information in a readable format without compromising the key ideas passed down from the worlds of anthropology, child development, pediatrics and education. I hope you will find the information about a particular age immediately useful, and will also be captured by the obvious patterns of development. By tying what we know about children to what we know about school this volume fills an important niche in the parent or teacher library.

# Acknowledgments

I have been blessed during my years as a classroom teacher and teacher educator to collaborate with many gifted and dedicated colleagues. I would like to acknowledge the insight of several teachers who, over the years, have shared their struggles and observations and opened their classrooms to inquiry and shared exploration on how to nurture a better classroom. Particularly, Marlynn Clayton and Deborah Porter, with whom I have shared two schools, the teaching of my own children and the teaching of other teachers. It has been a privilege to journey beside them.

Also, Ruth Charney, Marion Finer, Paula Denton, Roxann Kriete, and Ellen Doris, with whom I have shared classrooms, and Center School co-founder, Jay Lord — they have all taught me much about the art of teaching. Ruth Charney's skill in managing a classroom with intelligence, humor and deep respect for the lives of all children has been a constant source of inspiration for me. Also, I extend my gratitude to all the other teachers at the Center School, who over the past sixteen years have persisted in their dedication to exploration and change on behalf of children, as well as to all the parents at the Center School who have shown a strong commitment to a broader mission in education.

In Washington, DC, I remain indebted to Maurice Sykes, Linda Harrison, Barbara Nophlin, Mary Duru, Kathleen Thomas, Austine Fowler, and Myrtle Lewis for believing in our work and to a large number of classroom teachers who have opened their doors, including Joyce Love, Stephanie Abney and all the teachers at Garrison Elementary and their Principal, Andrea Irby-Robinson; Sheila Ford, Principal, and all of the fine staff at Horace Mann Elementary. Our work in classrooms today — from Chicago and Cincinnati to Cortland, NY, from Minneapolis, MN, to Milo, Maine — has enhanced my understanding of the difficult issues teachers and children face in a rapidly changing world. These are but a few of the places — each classroom, each workshop, each child encountered has made me a better teacher. I am grateful for each moment.

I would especially like to acknowledge my deep appreciation to Jackie Haines, currently Director of Gesell Institute, who served as my mentor in child development and patiently taught me to see with new eyes.

Thanks to the insightful and supportive editorial guidance of Roxann Kriete, this expanded edition is clearer, more readable and more helpful to parents and teachers. Thanks also to the children and teachers of the Greenfield Center School for their bibliographies of favorite and useful books as well as self-portraits, especially Librarian Chris Pinney. Thanks to Jay Lord and Ruth Charney for material on subject area content for ages 13-14. Sandy Yager's help with bringing this manuscript to production is appreciated.

Thanks also to my own family — Elizabeth Wood, my mother; my late father, Robert L. Wood; and my sister, Claudia Rahm — who taught me to care for others.

Finally, to my wife, Reenie, and my two children, Jon and Heather, who have shared me generously with so many children and families over the years — thank you for your love and support.

*Yardsticks* is not a definitive work, but a defining effort. Like a dictionary or thesaurus, it can provide reference but understanding can only be obtained in the context of your own search for meaning about children's growth and development.

I am sure most of you are captivated, as I am, by the ultimate magic and mysteries of childhood. I also share with you a deep and abiding reverence for the clear, honest vision of the children themselves. I believe it is our duty to protect and nourish that vision through our teaching and parenting. I hope that *Yardsticks* helps you in this effort.

Robert (Chip) Wood
Greenfield, Massachusetts
January, 1997

# Introduction

In 1978, after six years as an elementary school teacher and teaching principal, I attended a workshop on child development sponsored by Gesell Institute. That one day changed forever my view of education. Suddenly, I saw the children instead of the school; the lives to be lived, not just the lessons to be learned. Reading and math became contextual, rich with the particular developmental understanding that children brought to the subject matter at different ages. I vowed to learn more. Over the past eighteen years I have directed my professional efforts toward understanding the context of learning and passing on this knowledge to teachers.

My approach to child development is a mixture of theory and practice, reading and observation, repetition and reflection, sifted through my own experience as child, parent, teacher, administrator and teacher educator. The works of Piaget, Gesell, Erikson, Montessori, Rudolph Steiner, Caroline Pratt, Lucy Sprague Mitchell, Dorothy Cohen, Louise Bates Ames, and others provided me with a foundation for my observations;

they helped me to understand some of the behaviors and characteristics I was seeing each day of every school year.

In 1985, with my colleagues Ruth Charney, Marlynn Clayton, Marion Finer and Jay Lord, I helped to write the first book published by the Northeast Foundation for Children, *A Notebook for Teachers: Making Changes in the Elementary Curriculum*. In that book I charted the developmental characteristics of children from ages five to seven, using the works of Gesell, Piaget and Erikson as primary references. Since that time, I have deliberately sought to broaden my knowledge through direct observation in the classroom as well as expanded reading of other and more diverse theoreticians. The classic child development research confronted me with some common difficulties: it was largely focused on the white world of middle class children and much of it was over forty years old.

*Raising Black Children* and other works by African American psychiatrists James Comer and Alvin Poussaint and *Childhood: A Multicultural View* by Melvin Konner are current resources which provide invaluable insight into the growth of children of African American, Latino, and Asian descent. Beyond these sources, I have found there is not a great deal available to teachers and parents which is written on a popular level. One author who *has* bridged the fields of child development, education and anthropology is Barbara Rogoff. Her book, *Apprenticeship in Thinking,* has been an invaluable resource in my growing interest in social interaction, social skills development and the classroom.

For this edition of *Yardsticks*, I have included the charts for ages four through twelve and have added ages thirteen and fourteen to include characteristics of all middle school years. I have drawn on many more sources, including the actual observations of hundreds of children by scores of teachers over the past twenty years, to create this continuum. For this edition, I interviewed teenagers in both rural and urban settings to gain their perspective on their own developmental issues. I am fully aware that I have had to be selective in culling the developmental characteristics that seem to be most indicative of a particular age.

It is also important, as I will note here and often, that you understand the limitations of these characteristics — they are general expectations that help us gain an appreciation for the patterns of development rather than standards or precise predictions of what will happen at a given age. Culture, environment, health, temperament, and personality all affect the make-up of every child at every age. It is helpful that certain patterns have emerged and been documented, but they are never absolute. As Melvin Konner writes in *Childhood*, "We have to be patient; we are finding out new things just as fast as we know how. And if anyone gives you the impression that he has the answers now to the great timeless questions about childhood, you can smile and listen politely or you can turn your back and walk away, but in any case don't believe him."

I want to be clear that this book does not present answers, but snapshots of development. They are based on observations in the classroom — mine and many other teachers — and the observations of the great theorists in many settings at many different points in history.

# Developmental Issues Affecting All Children

Children's developmental needs should be the foundation for every choice we make in our classrooms and schools. They need to remain at the center of our decisions about school organization, policies, scheduling, and everyday practices. Too often, our choices affect children negatively, interfering with growth and learning rather than encouraging it. If we understand children's developmental needs more fully, we can change — and improve — our schools. Here are some suggestions on issues that are often overlooked or misunderstood.

## Mixed-Age Groupings

From the one-room schoolhouse to the assembly-line model of single-age grades, America's schools have tried many ways to group students. Most traditional classrooms contain a single grade of children, but because of chronological differences and standard academic retention policies, the ages of children will typically vary by as much as two years in such groupings.

In the 1990's there is a renewed interest in mixed-age groupings of children, largely in the primary grades. A great deal of attention is being focused on classrooms where children between six and nine years of age work in heterogeneous groupings and progress academically according to their own needs, timetables and abilities. This approach was also tried in so-called "open classroom" schools in the 1960's and 70's and during the progressive era of education in the 1930's and early 1940's.

There is much to be said for mixed-age *learning* in schools: children can gain a great deal from teaching younger children; younger children have much to learn from reaching up for new knowledge and modeling older children. But mixed-age teaching poses distinct challenges.

I taught in a mixed-age primary (grades 1, 2, 3) setting for three years in the 1970's and had the opportunity to see children's progress in such a program. There was no question that the children enjoyed the social mix of ages much of the time and that they found the mix of activities stimulating. However, it became clear to me and my colleagues that it was nearly impossible to keep up with the children's academic needs, given the wide span of abilities. A lovely environment for the children created burn-out for a group of highly motivated and conscientious teachers.

The academic needs of all the children were clearly not being met. Parents were rightly concerned about whether older children were being challenged and whether the youngest children could keep up. After another twenty years of classroom experience, my colleagues and I have settled on two premises for grouping children:

1. The maximum range for even the most talented teachers is about a three-year chronological and two-year grade spread.

2. It's extremely important for teachers to have the opportunity to stay with the same group of children for two years in a row.

The practice of moving children every year from one adult to another was based on Henry Ford's model for building cars. Today we know that model may not even be the best for

MARLYNN CLAYTON

building automobiles. It certainly is not the best for building successful students. Teachers who have the opportunity to teach the same children for two years in a row report a number of benefits. They know their students' strengths and weaknesses better at the beginning of the second year. Less time is needed for classroom management and learning expectations (although with developmental changes there will be different issues to deal with in the second year). Parents also report greatly improved relationships with teachers concerning the "shared" youngster.

## Some Suggestions on Grouping

Certain ages of children seem to do better together than others, based on a number of different two-year groupings in our laboratory school. For instance, five and six year old children work extremely well together, which makes kindergarten and first grade a good, all-day mix. In our opinion, the first grade environment should be just like kindergarten, allowing sixes as well as fives to learn in an activity-based program.

Fours and fives, on the other hand, have a harder time in mixed-age settings because of the completely active, outdoor, gross motor orientation of fours. They truly do need to spend the majority of their day climbing, swinging, digging and running!

Sevens seem to thrive when they are left alone. This "age of transition" is characterized by a need for privacy, by great sensitivity and often moodiness. The constant chatter and busy activity of sixes can be highly distracting to sevens.

Although sevens will often compare themselves negatively to more competent eights, they will still do better with older than with younger children in a mixed-age group. We have settled on a single second grade group, knowing that there will be sevens and eights in the class.

Third and fourth grade children (ages eight and nine) can work well in a mixed-age setting. The academic spread seems wide to many teachers, but we have also seen it work extremely well. Recently our teachers have chosen to spend one year with the third graders and then move with them to fourth grade. This way the teacher has the children for two years, but in single-grade groups.

Fifth and sixth grade groupings (ages ten and eleven) are highly effective and tend to make the struggles at school less intense for the eleven and new twelve year olds. The tens are more settled and school-compliant and can help provide a calmer, more reasonable transition into the middle school years for the older children.

Seventh and eighth graders (ages twelve and thirteen) also work well together in mixed-age settings, although the eighth graders tend to create their own space and privileges. They also can provide highly effective role models for the seventh graders who are generally less mature in their behavior. Jay Lord, a master middle grades teacher and co-founder of the Greenfield Center School, has long believed in the benefits of groups combining sixth through eighth grades. His experience shows that the older children provide even more useful role models for the sixth grade students.

Few middle schools (even those with "team" approaches) are yet utilizing even two year spreads in grouping children. Most, however, are finally grouping children heterogeneously instead of in homogeneous ability groupings.

## Normal Differences in Development

No matter how children are grouped chronologically or by grade, there will also always be a wide spread in normal developmental differences. A two year span in development is normal in any area of a child's development — physical, social, language or cognitive growth. Thus, a child who is ten years old chronologically may still be exhibiting social behaviors more typical of a nine year old. A five year old may display the physical prowess of a six year old. A seven year old child may be reading at a fifth grade level, but have trouble making friends like other seven year olds.

Personality plays a clear and often dramatic role in the way children move through developmental stages, too. Shy and quiet children will move through their childhood one way, loud and active children another. It is very important to remember that each child is an individual: his or her development will be unique even though it fits within a broad developmental pattern. The "yardsticks" in this book are not standards to be lived up to, but indicators to help guide the way.

# Racial and Cultural Considerations

As indicated in the Preface, most of the research on patterns of child growth and development which is easily accessible to parents and teachers is the result of studies of white children by white researchers, and much of that research is dated. This does not invalidate the storehouse of knowledge that has been gained from this work (which is the foundation for this book and many others), but it should encourage us to reach for additional data from research with other racial and ethnic populations.

Several variables affect the growth and development of African American, Latino, Asian, and Native American children in American schools and in general. Bertha Garrett Holliday (1985) has summarized into five categories the ways in which both the process and content of African American children's development differs from that of white children. It might be extrapolated that this is also true for other non-white children as well, although Garrett Holliday does not make such an assertion. This excerpt from "Developmental Imperatives of Social Ecologies" appearing in *Black Children* (McAdoo and McAdoo, 1985) details her five categories:

1. The ecological structure of Black children's lives is more complex than that of white children. Black children's interactions with both Black and white communities result in their potential involvement in more settings.

2. Relationships between white and Black communities are defined by patterns of domination and subordination and punctuated by differences in values, social relations and institutional patterns. Therefore, Black children who must

interact with both communities, are confronted with more role requirements that are qualitatively more varied.

3. Variations in role requirements within Black and white communities coupled with systematic social barriers cause Black children to develop skills appropriate for effecting transitions within both white and Black communities as well as between the two. Black children therefore must develop more extensive behavior repertoires that must be demonstrated with greater flexibility in anticipation of more problematic situations.

4. Relationships between Black and white communities result in Blacks having less access to and reduced control of schedules and contingencies of reward. Consequently, Black children frequently are unable to predict if their efforts in problematic situations will be associated with success or failure. This lack of probability is double-edged in its developmental consequences. On one hand, it provides Black children opportunities for that kind of sweet success against the odds that undergirds exceptional competence. But it also provides them opportunities for that kind of unexpected, mystifying, paralyzing failure that overwhelms children and leads them to assume postures of stagnation, indifference and hostility.

5. Black children are older younger. Their experiences in bicultural settings encourage that kind of social-cognitive and behavioral precocity ("motherwit") that spurs earlier maturity and independence.

◆ ◆ ◆

While *basic* developmental expectations may be similar for all children in all cultures, Garrett Holliday clearly points out that African American children must face a much more complex array of developmental tasks as they grow up than white children. She also suggests that this "ecological structure" can have either a positive or negative impact on the course of development for African American children. In either case, African American children may present older social and adaptive behavior than their white counterparts. It's important to keep this in mind when reading this book and weighing developmental expectations for children in African American families.

The respected author of *Black Children: Their Roots, Culture and Learning Styles* (1982), Janice Hale-Benson, in her own work and in surveying a number of studies, emphasizes that the disproportionately lowered achievement for African Americans (especially for African American males) is primarily a function of the way they are perceived

and treated by their teachers, rather than a function of home or community environment. Many researchers, she notes, have documented the fact that teachers expect more from and value the school behaviors of white females, white males, Black females and Black males, in that order.

The difference between the culture of school and the culture of the African American family and community creates conflicting and often self-defeating messages for young students. Again, in reading the "Classroom Implications" for children at various ages as charted in this book, the reader is advised to take into account these critical warnings about racial and cultural bias in the school environment.

While I do believe that the general expectations and considerations I have described in this book apply to most children, I also firmly believe that there are a host of additional considerations and expectations that must be taken into account. It is incumbent on all teachers to become aware of these factors. I can recommend no better place to start than the work of Janice Hale-Benson.

## Ability Grouping

"Research has shown . . ." How many times have we read that statement and wondered, "Whose research? What other research shows just the opposite?" Nowhere is research more politically sensitive than in the field of ability grouping. The history of American education is filled with examples of the misuse of ability grouping in schools as a way to enforce racial and cultural separation and to reinforce the racial stereotypes discussed in the previous section.

CHERRY WYMAN

## Tracking

Ability grouping, or "tracking" as it is more commonly known, has traditionally been the means of dividing children by "intelligence" and social class and determining which children would continue formal education through high school and beyond. Although the United States has the most universal education in the world, ability grouping often restricts children from further education rather than encouraging them.

Ability grouping is *extremely* detrimental to young children and a questionable practice at any age right through high school. In kindergarten through sixth grade, it has been common to separate children into different classes according to their basic reading abilities. Fortunately, many schools are finally moving away from this procedure. Such grouping tells children right away what the pecking order is at school, who will make it and who won't, who is in, who is out.

The message is not subtle and it wrongly focuses on only one skill. Children with exceptional math ability or musical ability or scientific reasoning or artistic ability, but with low or merely slowly-developing reading ability are shuttled into low-ability tracks where their natural gifts are often depressed or disappear completely because those abilities are also taught at a pace for a lower track.

Some methods of ability grouping are still very common. In one form, called the "Joplin Plan," children are assigned to mixed-ability homerooms, but then go to different teachers for instruction, returning to their homerooms at the end of the day. In other forms, children go to different teachers as early as first grade for their reading and math instruction and then are separated into ability groups within these subject sections. This was popular in the 1950's and is reappearing in many schools at younger grade levels than ever before.

I also believe that the middle school model of grouping children by ability and moving them to new teachers every 50 minutes is contrary to the key developmental struggle of the age — the deep need for belonging and identity. Schools that are working on "team" grouping of students seem to me to be on the right track — one group of teachers works with 100-150 children through the entire school year. In these schools, teachers have greater flexibility in organizing the daily schedule. They can make time for trips, community service, cooperative learning projects and "advisories" or homerooms where students can work on social issues, student council, clubs and other peer activities.

Heterogeneously grouped, these teams (or "houses") establish a close identity of their own. They can encourage democratic values in students and work against the apathy and cynicism so prevalent at this age. Some high schools are also successfully utilizing this approach to school organization and heterogenous ability grouping.

## Inclusion

On the other end of the spectrum is the "inclusion" model. Special teachers or assistants are brought into the regular classroom to help children of various levels (both "gifted" and "remedial" or "disabled") and to help the regular teacher monitor progress. This plan has the greatest potential for respecting the self-worth of each learner. It also maintains the "primary caregiver" model where the lead teacher remains with her group of children for the majority of the day. In elementary school, this approach is certainly the most sensitive to the developmental needs of children in all aspects of their development — physical, social, and cognitive.

# Retention

The practice of "retention" (keeping children back a year in school) has been one of the most controversial subjects in education over the past thirty years. Today, it is commonly agreed that retaining a child because of academic failure and having them "repeat" the grade and subject material will usually not produce the desired results: catching up academically and succeeding in school. Most of the research indicates failure for those children who do repeat. For those who repeat two years, the eventual outcome is often dropping out of school altogether.

This practice has affected disproportionately large numbers of African American and Latino children. On the other hand, there are those children who, for developmental rather than academic reasons, will benefit by an extra year of school in order to progress with their social, emotional, and physical peers. This may be a small percentage of children, but there is no question that for them a longer period of maturation in school (as well as life) will be to their benefit.

Schools must be cautious about the way in which the determination for extra year placement is made and should involve parents every step of the way. An extra year in school should *never* be for purely academic reasons, no matter what the age. *If a child is retained for academic reasons, it is the school that has failed the child, not the other way around.* Academic differences can be accommodated in school much more easily than wide differences in developmental maturity. Although mixed-age groupings are currently popular, they aren't likely to be a viable solution if too wide of a range of developmental ages and academic skills are included. (See the section on mixed-age groupings)

The verb "retain" can mean to hold back or to hold safe. Educators and parents should carefully examine the difference when contemplating extra time in school for the individual child.

MARLYNN CLAYTON

# Food

All children have a need for food beyond three square meals a day. In fact, children's needs for nourishment often seem to come at any time *except* the time scheduled for breakfast, lunch, or dinner. Early childhood educators have long recognized the need for preschool, kindergarten and early primary children to have a snack in school. Many of us fondly remember milk and straws and graham crackers from our earliest school years.

Many early childhood classrooms have moved beyond the practice of stopping the entire class at a certain time each morning for a half hour snack period. Instead, a snack table is set up in one area of the room and children learn to manage and regulate their own needs for a snack. The class accomplishes more during a morning without interruption, and snack becomes an integral part of the social and academic curriculum.

All ages of children will benefit from having a snack (or snacks) in their school day. Unfortunately, snack usually ends in first or second grade, replaced with the rule: NO FOOD ALLOWED IN THE CLASSROOM. In fact, the lack of snack contributes to poor attention, concentration and attitude. The eight year old who becomes easily fatigued can bounce back with a little nourishment. The eleven year old who seems out of sorts can refocus on the task at hand after a handful of popcorn. Obviously, sweets and junk food are to be discouraged (or banned outright) because they can contribute to excess nervous energy. But it is counterproductive to prevent snacks for older children in school.

Some teachers simply tell children and parents that snack is allowed and can be packed with lunch. For those who take hot lunch, a snack can be packed separately. For those on low budgets, a bag of pretzels or some fruit goes a long way; for those on no budgets, teachers usually keep their own stash of pretzels in the closet. Rules and regulations are necessary to make eating in the classroom work, but when they are generated in cooperation with the children, they are rarely abused. If they are, snack can be removed for a few days and reinstated after a review of expectations.

The developmental issue is clear: food is a major ingredient in children's daily needs. Hunger does not follow a school schedule. A child's inability to pay attention may be rectified by a simple snack. As a parent or a teacher, the next time you pick up that mid-morning cup of coffee, think about your kids and the food policy at school. Parents can talk about the issue to the teachers and principal at school by placing it on the agenda of a school-wide PTO meeting. Principals can consult lunch programs to see what kind of snacks can be provided under the law. State lunch program administrators can examine free breakfast and lunch policies and practices for possible adjustments.

# Exercise

I am amazed at the number of schools I visit where a morning or afternoon recess is a thing of the past. In many schools, children are lucky if they get twenty minutes of outdoor play each day. Formal physical education is often limited to one hour per week. Faculty and administrators say they place these severe restrictions on children's growing bodies because there is just too much work to do in school and not enough time to do it. In some locations, children are kept indoors because administrators say they can't guarantee children's safety on the playground. The "weather forecast" approach is common as well: a degree too cold or too hot, a drop of rain or a fine mist can bring the announcement over the PA system, "Teachers are advised that there will be indoor recess today."

Like food, all children need frequent exercise. Oxygen is food for the brain and nine year olds need it just as much as four year olds. Even a five or ten minute break to run around the school building or to jump rope in the side yard can make a huge difference in the way children feel and perform in the classroom. Even inside the room, a break to do "Head and Shoulders, Knees and Toes," aerobics to music, or five minutes of the latest dance craze can improve attention and attitude. Teachers need the physical exercise — we need oxygen flowing

to our brains, too! It helps make us more cheerful and engaging.

Sunlight and air are as important to our growth as to the plants and trees. If you teach in a school without windows, or your children attend one, insist that the children be taken outside at least twice a day. Many discipline problems in school can be traced directly to the lack of physical activity. Growing numbers of children diagnosed as ADD or ADHD (or other hyperactive labels) desperately need physical release in their school day. Academic proficiency will increase for these children (and all children) with an increase in physical activity, not the other way around.

## The School Day

Years ago, the brilliant educator Sylvia Ashton-Warner taught us about the daily rhythms of classroom life in her classic book, *Teacher* (1971). Today, our school schedules don't always pay close attention to the pace of childhood or the changing developmental needs of children. Consider, for instance, recess after lunch. Haven't we got it backwards? Doesn't it make more sense to work up an appetite, then have a quiet rest period after lunch, rather than eat and then go right out and run around? Schools that have reorganized their schedules to allow for this simple change find a difference in the behaviors and energy levels of their children in the afternoon.

At the Greenfield Center School, the laboratory school of Northeast Foundation for Children, a half hour quiet time follows lunch in most classes. Children are free to rest, read, draw, do homework, whatever they want — but they must do it by themselves and they may not speak or move around the room during this half hour. An active afternoon of learning follows.

We have also found that children from kindergarten to sixth grade work well in the morning in blocks ranging from a half hour to forty-five minutes, devoting themselves to different interests or subject matter in each block. But in the afternoon, longer and more leisurely stretches of time allow more productive learning. As in many other schools, the morning is usually devoted to writing, reading and mathematics, the afternoon to theme work (social studies and science).

In most schools, special subjects like art, music and physical education are confined to half hour blocks, but children would benefit from longer periods (just as they do in the afternoon for social studies or science). Limited budgets, lack of personnel, and concentration on what are seen as "the basics" often diminish this possibility. In the Center School, there is no budget for special subject teachers. But longer periods for art, music and physical education are integrated into the thematic studies chosen by teachers at each grade level (see Curriculum section).

## Transitions

It is increasingly common to switch children from one teacher to another for reading, math, social studies, science — and it's usually the *children* who move from one room to another. From a developmental perspective, this is a questionable practice. Many middle school schedules look like a mini-high school.

Our experience indicates that the most important variable in a positive elementary school program is the constant attention of a single teacher/caregiver with whom the child can develop a predictable and meaningful relationship. As children reach the ages of eleven and twelve, peers become more important and teachers less important to the children. But especially in these first stages of independence, children need one teacher there as an anchor, as well as an object for rebellion.

As children work within our scheduled time blocks, we must be careful to honor the pace of childhood. We must not hurry children. This does not mean that we cannot stop them at the end of a period and move them on to another activity, but it does mean that we need to be sensitive to the way we help

children move from one thing to another. "Hurry up children, it's time for gym; hurry up children, it's time for spelling; hurry up children, it's time for music." Early childhood expert Jackie Haines tells the story of one kindergarten teacher who knew she'd had enough when she heard herself say, "Hurry up children, it's time to rest."

A quiet, individual reminder for a seven year old can make all the difference in the world: "Don't forget, we have to be cleaned up for gym in five minutes." In kindergarten, a gentle bell sounds and the teacher says, "In five minutes we will be ending our working period. Think about what you need to do to be finished." It's important, in our distracted adult world, to remember that children become deeply absorbed in the important business of learning and growing. We need to help them manage this process rather than drag them helter-skelter through a hectic day.

Children's sense of time and their level of absorption varies with age. The familiar teacher's words, "Put your work down children, we'll finish that when we come back from music," will be met by different behavior at different ages. The sixes are likely to be quickly lined up and ready to go out the door (with their work still scattered at their desks) because they are six year olds and love to be first. The seven year old is likely to put up her hand and say, "Teacher, I've just got one more problem to do, can't I finish it?" The need for closure at seven often overrides the need to move on.

Being sensitive to these developmental differences can help teachers adjust daily schedules, especially the amount of time needed for transitions. This is also true for parents as they think about the time it will take to get out the door in the morning or get a bath and a story on the way to bed.

## Child Care

Many children are now in some form of child care away from their parents from early in the morning until 5 or 6 PM. Because of the changing nature of our society and the needs of families with a single parent or both parents employed, many schools are beginning to provide care after school. Again, a constant caregiver with a minimum of transitions should be the goal. In general, young children's sense of themselves in the world will be more stable and secure the less time they spend being shuffled from one setting to another.

## Yearly Calendar

As society changes, the school calendar is also coming under increased scrutiny. Today, we still use the agrarian calendar which worked so well for children and families when the major consideration was planting and reaping. But there is little question that it is of no practical use in American society today and, in fact, works against the best interest of children's academic growth and development. Most schools in the United States operate on a 180 day calendar. Children spend half a year in school and half a year . . . on vacation?

Twenty-four other countries have longer school years than we do. Japanese schoolchildren go to school 243 days a year, including half a day on Saturdays. Academic achievement may not be directly correlated to the amount of time spent in school — there are many variables — but we rank below most countries with longer school years on most standard measures.

Although there is a great deal of resistance to changing the school calendar, a growing movement for "year round school" is gaining momentum. It may begin to influence education if the few major experiments (largely in California) should prove successful.

# Curriculum

At the end of each age chapter, curriculum charts offer a subject-at-a-glance look at the developmental continuum between ages four and fourteen. Remember that age and cognitive growth do not necessarily go hand in hand. Some children, for instance, will be ready for reading instruction at earlier ages than others while some children may not be ready to read until past the "expected" age. Schools are often very quick to label such children learning disabled or remedial when enrichment and language experience may be the key to success. On the other hand, schools steeped in a whole language tradition can wait too long with some children to begin intervention strategies (such as "Reading Recovery") that can be very helpful.

A good rule of thumb is to do some diagnostic work at the end of first grade if the six or soon-to-be seven year old is frustrated and struggling with whatever reading approach is in place. A similar approach is recommended for the acquisition of basic mathematical concepts of counting, simple measurement, beginning addition and subtraction, and grouping or "set making."

Included in the writing charts you will find information about the developmental continuum in writing, spelling, thematic interests of young writers and their usual handwriting approach. Again, remember that development in these areas does not always correspond neatly to a specific chronological age. Writing, spelling and thematic interest are tied to the cognitive development of children; handwriting is related to both cognitive and physical development.

The teaching of themes (Social Studies, Science, Current Events) is currently extremely popular and has been a common instructional method throughout the history of education. "Unit Teaching," for instance, was a well known and widely used approach in the thirties, forties and fifties. Theme study allows teachers to integrate subject matter and varied skill development (such as in art, music) into the regular curriculum, rather than limiting such instruction to special subject teachers. Nowhere is this more important than in teaching cultural and ethnic diversity, which should permeate all subject areas.

Some of the pitfalls with thematic instruction can be a lack of continuity leading to gaps in content knowledge from grade to grade and the choosing of themes that bear little relationship to the developmental interests of children. At the Greenfield Center School we try to combine a "concentric circle" model of themes (as first introduced by Lucy Sprague Mitchell in the 1930's) with teacher and student interest. This allows us to focus on experiential and concrete knowledge. For example, children build relief maps rather than drawing them on paper, and use a compass in the woods rather than the classroom. The end-of-chapter charts list some typical themes by age.

These charts are not exhaustive — such as so-called "scope and sequence" charts often found in formal curricula — and they *do* express the curriculum biases of a developmentally appropriate continuum as practiced at the Greenfield Center School and in my own career as a teacher.

## Major Developmental Considerations

There is wide agreement about certain patterns in children's growth and development. Most of these are credited to the so-called "giants" in the field like Piaget, Gesell, Erikson, and

Vygotsky. But these patterns have been validated over the years by numerous academic research studies, anthropologists studying children across the world and across time, and teachers and parents who have corroborated theory through the practice of teaching and parenting, scolding and loving. Pick up a good college text for an introductory course in child development and these patterns will be defined in detail.

Theories change and are constantly questioned, as researchers gain new knowledge and understanding. Here are a few of the ideas that, thus far, have stood the test of time.

1. Children's growth and development follow reasonably predictable patterns. There are patterns in physical maturation, language acquisition, social behavior and cognition or thinking. These patterns have been broken down into defined stages in different ways according to particular theories. Each stage is defined by certain changes in growth patterns and ways of approaching the world that seem to be relatively universal.

2. Growth is deeply influenced by culture, personality and environment. No two children are the same, no two families, no two communities. While children may all go through predictable stages in the same order, they will not all go through them at the same rate. *Normal* differences in development can span two chronological years. Racial and cultural differences also influence development.

3. Development and intelligence do not proceed at the same rate. A very bright youngster can mature slowly in physical and social development. A child of average or

below average "intelligence" may be ahead in physical and social development. Intelligence in music, mechanical ability, or the arts may move ahead of more traditional "intelligence" in common school learning.

4. Growth is uneven. Like the seasons, the tides, the turning of the earth on itself and around the sun, the birth and death of stars, the music of the universe — there is an ebb and flow to life that is mystical and spiritual. Babies are calm at one time of day, fretful at another. Children are more compliant and obedient at one age, more resistant and difficult at others. Learning seems to come in spurts and be followed by periods of consolidation. Sudden spurts of physical growth are obvious, and are followed by periods of little physical change. This shifting back and forth is a normal part of the life cycle and appears to continue into adulthood. Of course, changes are closer together in infancy and less frequent as we become older.

The "yardsticks" that follow combine research, theory and practice. They can help us understand what our children are going through without limiting them or burdening them with unrealistic expectations. Although the patterns are universal, each child is unique — each child a gift, each child a surprise.

# Yardsticks

All the world's a stage
And all the men and women merely players:
They have their exits and their entrances;
And one man in his time plays many parts
His acts being seven ages. At first the infant,
Mewling and puking in the nurse's arms.
And then the whining school-boy, with his satchel
And shining morning face, creeping like snail
Unwilling to school.

William Shakespeare, *As You Like It*, Act II, Scene vi

# Four Year Olds

*"Give me my Bunny!" he said*
*"You musn't say that. He isn't a toy. He's REAL!"*

The Velveteen Rabbit
*by Margery Williams*

When my own son was four years old we lived on a paved country road that saw occasional, but speedy traffic. One Saturday morning, a worried motorist knocked on the door. "Do you have a little boy and a dog? If you do, they're a half mile up the road and moving fast." The yard gate had been opened by intelligent fingers for the first time and boy and dog had made their escape into the world. Fortunately, we retrieved them safely, changed the gate lock, and continued our education of, and by, the four year old. Some parents lose exploring children between parked cars, out open windows or off fire escapes. Our story, too, could have had a different ending.

Fours are ready for everything. They are explorers and adventurers and are soaking up the world of knowledge with incredible speed. They are capable of almost nonstop mental

and physical gymnastics. Parents and teachers need vast amounts of energy to keep up with these young dynamos.

Four year olds are present in our public school classrooms, not just in prekindergarten and Headstart. Many school districts have policies that admit children who turn five before December 31 of a given school year. Thus, many kindergartens have children still four or four and a half when they enter kindergarten, and three or three and a half when they begin a prekindergarten or Headstart program. Children at four demand school programs which are flexible, exciting and creative because they are flexible, exciting and creative creatures. They respond joyfully to dance, creative movement, outdoor play, and drama.

Children love to exaggerate at four. A tall tale about a villain who followed him home from nursery school may worry a parent or teacher, but not the four year old. Short attention spans match their short bodies. Headstart, prekindergarten *and* kindergarten programs must reflect this characteristic. Activity centers (or areas of the room) are generally arranged so fours can move from center to center or area to area across the room without a lot of traffic congestion. Four's vision looks toward the horizon, and these traffic patterns minimize accidents and knock-overs.

Paper and pencil tasks should be kept to a minimum for four year olds in preschool *and* in kindergarten. They learn best through their own play, by being read to, by acting out stories and fairy tales, by manipulating clay, paint brushes, finger paints, building blocks, math materials. Outdoor play is also essential for fours; they should spend at least a quarter of their school day in physical activity. This is an age where much learning is transmitted through the large muscles. *Learning goes from the hand to the head, not the other way around.* Teachers in four year old classrooms need to focus on observing and redirecting behavior, and asking questions that lead children toward the next level of cognitive exploration and understanding.

# The Four Year Old: Growth Patterns

**Physical**
- Vision in the far field, on the horizon
- Sometimes appear clumsy, awkward; spills and accidents common
- Hand and fingers an extension of whole arm; i.e., fine motor skills not dominant
- Fisted pencil grasp typical
- Enjoy much physical activity — running, jumping, climbing
- Can sit still for only brief periods

**Social**
- Friendly, gregarious, chatty, "bubbly" age
- Love working with their friends, but still much parallel play
- Move quickly from one thing to the next, short attention span
- Can make decisions based on interest; not overly dependent on adults, though obviously requiring their guidance
- Like responsibility of a "big person" job (setting the table, folding the clothes, putting out the snack)
- Older fours sometime fearful, worried; nightmares

# The Four Year Old: Growth Patterns

**Language**
- Expansive; enjoy using big words, trying out language
- Bathroom language often evident, as well as other "swears"
- *Very* talkative; likes to explain: ". . . and you know what, teacher? . . ."
- Loves being read to

**Cognitive**
- Learn best through play and exploration — "hand to head"
- Like to imitate adult roles through imaginative play — dress up, dramatic play
- Music and rhythm, repeating patterns — simple learning strategies
- Learn more through large muscles than small — i.e., hauling blocks, easel painting rather than paper/pencil task

# The Four Year Old in the Classroom
### Headstart — Prekindergarten — Beginning Kindergarten

| | |
|---|---|
| **Vision and Fine Motor Ability** | • "Close" visual activity (reading, writing) kept to a minimum and for short periods<br>• Use whole hand to write, printing usually large<br>• *Never* have children copy from board |
| **Gross Motor Ability** | • Learning through large muscle activity & play<br>• Need climbing apparatus on the playground<br>• Easel and finger painting excellent for pre-writing; stand-up easel important for vision<br>• Big blocks, "hollow" blocks allow for construction using large muscles<br>• Tumbling is usually successful in phys. ed. |
| **Cognitive Growth** | • Love being read to — individually, small groups, whole class; love to do their own "reading" in picture books<br>• Constantly reading the environment — label objects frequently seen or used (not all objects randomly)<br>• Manipulative experiences important in many areas of room — magnets, pullies in science area; puzzles, interlocking cubes in math; scoops, funnels, measuring cups in sand table, etc. |

# The Four Year Old in the Classroom
### *Headstart — Prekindergarten — Beginning Kindergarten*

**Cognitive Growth**

- Provide functional opportunities for counting such as attendance, milk count, boots and coats

- Don't expect children to stay in one area of room for extended time — learning is speedy

- Do expect clean-up at the end of work period, but model expectations (i.e., Montessori's "practical life" activities)

**Social Behavior**

- Learn from modeling; need chances to practice new or appropriate behavior

- Easily redirected from inappropriate behavior; teacher language all important to help children to use language instead of physical reaction — "Use words," "Tell her what you want," "Ask if he is through," etc.; small dramas and role plays help teach social skills

- Love to learn to work together, although parallel play may continue for younger fours; "Who's the boss?" often the major developmental issue; can learn basic mediation skills, but "It's the rule" works wonders

- Roughhouse play on the playground needs teacher redirection and modeling of appropriate behavior

# The Four Year Old: Curriculum

**Reading**
- Children love to be read to; especially enjoy picture books with repetitive themes
- "Parallel" reading with an adult; child "reads" one page (telling the familiar story), you read the next
- "Predictable" books with few words and repeating phrases, or books with pictures and no words help build the sequences of reading

**Writing**
- *Writing* — "scribble" writing and drawing predominate
- *Spelling* — Prephonemic — many letters do not correspond to sounds, i.e., BHKEEEEEEEJB for sailboat
- *Writing Themes* — Blood and gore; fantasy; TV take-offs; fairy tales; pets
- *Handwriting* — Tend to grasp pencil or crayon in a whole fist; young fours may hold pencil more tentatively toward eraser and write with a very light stroke; older fours are bolder and firmer with stroke

# The Four Year Old: Curriculum

**Thematic Units**

*(Social Studies, Science, Current Events)*

- Dinosaurs; all about me; transportation (cars, trucks, trains and planes); houses

**Mathematics**

- Exploration of size, shape, length, volume through experience with objects and materials such as blocks, cubes, interlocking blocks, sand, water, etc.
- Counting, sorting activities
- Math in stories

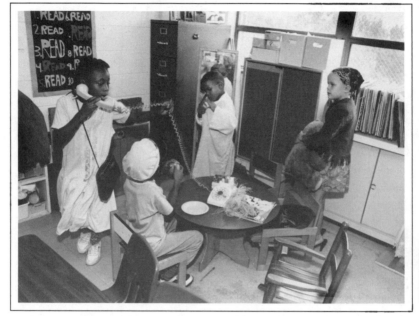

# Five Year Olds

*"Ramona loved Miss Binney so much she did not want to disappoint
her. Not ever. Miss Binney was the nicest teacher in the whole world."*

Ramona The Pest
*by Beverly Cleary*

After a busy morning in an overly academic kindergarten, a
five year old boy marched up to his teacher's desk, put his hands
on his hips and announced, "You don't seem to understand,
teacher, I just came here to eat and play!" Nothing could better
characterize the developmental needs of the five year old.
(Thanks to my colleague, Sue Sweitzer, for this story years ago.)

Gradually our kindergarten and first grade programs are
beginning to respond. The advent of "developmentally
appropriate programs" means that at least in kindergarten and
early primary grades, children are getting the opportunity to
play and learn in ways that respond to their levels of growth.

Learning is at its best for the five year old when it is both
structured and exploratory: structured through a clear and
predictable schedule; exploratory through carefully constructed

interest areas where children can initiate their own activity. The best teachers observe learning activities and create teacher-directed instruction to complement the children's interests and meet the learning expectations for the age.

Children move through two distinct developmental phases during the kindergarten year — one of caution, literalness and general compliance; a second of experimentation, oppositional behavior, and uncertainty. Some of these changes can be attributed to changing physical characteristics such as visual and perceptual changes (as in letter and number reversals). Others are related to changing cognitive patterns as children move from pre-operational learning, bounded by the senses, to new and more complex thinking patterns. This shift creates tension and disequilibrium.

Although many children have now been in social settings with peers outside the home for several years, kindergarten remains a time of immense social interest. Children love to explore the world of "real school" together. Fantasy play, dress-up, housekeeping, and puppets continue to be essential arenas for growth and development.

Five, overall, is a time of great happiness. Life is "good," says the five year old. A primary objective in life seems to be to please significant adults. Fives are constantly asking, "Mom, can I set the table? Can I put away the socks?" At school five year olds also ask permission. "Teacher, can I use these markers? Teacher, is this how you do it? How much can I use, teacher?"

The five year old needs the release of the adult to make transitions, move from task to task. Fives are literal and usually

accept adult rules as absolute and unbendable. In *Ramona the Pest* (Cleary, 1968), Ramona wouldn't budge from her seat the first day in kindergarten because her teacher told her to "sit here for the present." Ramona was sure she was going to get a present, not that she should sit in her place for *now*.

Children's vision is most easily focused on objects near to them. They become engrossed in the details of a block construction or a complicated painting. Because they lack the ability to sweep their eyes laterally, left-to-right and right-to-left, across a printed page with ease, most five year olds are not ready for formal reading instruction.

The young five year old seems in a period of consolidation, resting from the exuberant, somewhat wild behavior of four. At four the child exaggerated, told long stories, talked constantly and was always in motion. At five, they are a little calmer, more literal and exact. One word answers — "good" and "fine" — replace elaborate explanations. Parents may be frustrated with fives when they try to get answers to the question: "What did you do in school today?"

Five year olds are not selfish, but are at the center of their own universe and often find it hard to see the world from any other point of view. It may be impossible for children to complete a given task except in the one way they know — their way. They often have trouble expressing empathy if a conflict affects them directly — sharing their toys or space — but if a classmate across the room is crying, a crowd of caring fives may gather.

Typical behavior changes as children move through their fifth year. Visual and auditory confusions commonly show up in reversals of letters and numbers. The child is not sure which way things go and says so. "Yes and no" replaces "Yes!" An emphatic "NO" may remind us of the "terrible two's." Children are testing the limits they were so comfortable with a few months ago. Earlier in the year it was easier to sit still and listen. Now there are wiggles and complaints and it's not uncommon to see children falling sideways out of their chairs. (At six, they often fall over backwards.)

As children move toward six, their language becomes more differentiated and complex. They like to explain things and like to have things explained to them. Their behavior also becomes more complex. Children can play well one moment and argue the next. They may delight in independent activity or become instantly dependent on adult intervention. Sometimes they dawdle, sometimes they rush. Initiative drives them forward. The more they can do on their own, the stronger they feel. However, failure at any task may produce a strong sense of guilt. The balance between initiative and guilt provides the child with a feeling of purpose and worth. This purposefulness allows them to venture into a lengthy period of industriousness between the ages of six and eleven.

It is especially important to remember that five year olds do not think the same way about the world as adults do. Cause and effect are not explained through logic, but rather through intuition. Thought which appears illogical can be considered pre-logical — I go to sleep because it's night. Bound by the senses, restricted to what they can see, children must act on one thing at a time. The best kindergarten teachers know that they, too, must focus on one thing at a time, keeping expectations clear and simple.

# The Five Year Old: Growth Patterns

**Physical**
- Vision focused on objects close at hand
- Centered on task
- Gross motor control improving
- 3-fingered pincer grasp with pencil
- Falls out of chair sideways
- Paces self well
- Active but can control physical behavior

**Social**
- Likes to help; cooperative, wants to be "good"
- Likes rules and routines
- Needs approval
- Dependent on authority; wants to be told what to do, but also finds it difficult to see things from another's viewpoint

# The Five Year Old: Growth Patterns

**Language**
- Literal, succinct
- "Play" and "good" favorite words
- Needs release from adult — "Can I . . . ?"
- Fantasy is more active, less verbal
- Often does not communicate about school at home
- Thinks out loud

**Cognitive**
- Likes to copy
- Literal behavior; often only one way to do things
- Bound cognitively by sight and senses
- Animistic (inanimate objects have life, movement)
- Learns best through play and own action
- Does not yet think logically

# The Five Year Old in the Classroom
### Kindergarten — First Grade

**Vision and Fine Motor Ability**
- Tend to focus on one word at a time because visual tracking (left to right) not fully established
- Difficulty copying from blackboard or chart stand
- Beginning readers often need pointer or finger to keep place
- Reversals of letters and numbers (though few) need to be accepted, not corrected
- Manuscript printing can be *introduced*, but children should not be expected to stay within lines
- Difficulty spacing letters, numbers, and words; may need to use a finger to separate words

**Gross Motor Ability**
- Continued need for a great deal of active outdoor and indoor physical activity
- Good age for structured games — "Duck, Duck, Goose," "Red Light, Green Light," etc.

**Cognitive Growth**
- Repetitive behavior maximizes learning — repeat stories, poems, songs, games, sometimes with minor variations; patterning in math, science and daily scheduling important
- Encouragement an important release for children to move on to next task

# The Five Year Old in the Classroom
### Kindergarten — First Grade

**Cognitive Growth**

- Some become stuck in repetitive behavior (i.e., infinite rainbows and flowers) for fear of making mistake when trying something new
- Learn best through active exploration of concrete materials — blocks, manipulatives, paint, arts and crafts, sand and water, etc.
- Seldom able to see things from another's point of view

**Social Behavior**

- Can work at quiet, sitting activities for 15-20 minutes at a time
- Often need teacher's release to next task, though able to pace themselves within a given task
- Consistent guidelines, carefully planned periods help children feel safe
- Expect, allow children to think out loud — "I am going to move the truck!" precedes the action
- Dramatic play (housekeeping corner or dramatic play area) essential to language development; children can express thoughts through action
- Teacher modeling, directed role play provides chances to learn and practice language skills

# Changes as Children Move Toward Six

**Physical**
- Visual and auditory confusion
- Reversals common
- Physically restless
- Awkward fine motor skills
- Variable pencil grasp
- Tilts head to nondominant side
- Hand "gets tired" from firm grip
- Often stands up to do work
- Tires quickly

**Language**
- Equivocates — sometimes yes, sometimes no
- Elaborates and differentiates in answer to questions
- Verbal answers may not equal cognitive understanding; more words than ideas
- Auditory reversals (answers first what was heard last)

# Changes as Children Move Toward Six

**Social**
- Oppositional, not sure whether to be good or naughty
- Insecure with feelings
- Testing authority, limits
- Tentative
- Complains
- Temper tantrums; striking out
- Wonderful at home, terrible at school; or vice-versa

**Cognitive**
- Begins to try new activities more easily
- Makes lots of mistakes; recognizes some
- Learns well from direct experience

# The Older Five Year Old in the Classroom
### Kindergarten or First Grade

Many of the characteristics of five, of course, carry over as children move toward six. Increasingly unsettled behavior, however, is evidence of growth and change.

**Vision & Fine Motor Ability**
- Printing tends to be less neat than at five and with more reversals
- "Pencil grips" sometimes help with overly firm grasp
- Reversals of letters and numbers at their peak; reading and writing tasks can be extremely difficult and frustrating

**Gross Motor Ability**
- Need a good deal of physical activity; relaxed games or free play outside necessary because attention not always focused in structured gym class
- Tire quickly, sometimes necessitating shorter work periods than at five

# The Older Five Year Old in the Classroom
### Kindergarten or First Grade

**Cognitive Growth**

- Language still initiates action; begin to explain in more detail

- Need many avenues to express what they know — blocks, paints, arts and crafts, etc.

- Allow time to try out their own ways of doing things even when they sometimes get wrong answers; constantly validate their initiative

**Social Behavior**

- Consistent rules and discipline even more necessary than at five; harsh discipline (especially for mistakes) can be devastating because children are testing limits more

- Teacher's use of frequent questioning and redirecting works better now than at five

# The Five Year Old: Curriculum

**Reading**
- "Partner" reading can begin with peers helping each other through familiar books; early and more able readers often paired with more beginning readers, but both play an active role (as in "parallel" reading)
- Begin reading short chapter books to the class
- Big Books, and Language Experience stories written by the class and turned into Big Books a favorite activity
- "Predictable" books remain important
- Phonics instruction should be organic (given where and when needed), not formalized
- Encourage reading the environment — labels, signs, posters, charts

**Writing**
- *Writing* — Drawing and labeling with initial consonants to stand for one feature in the drawing; "stories" are told in a single drawing and one or two words
- *Spelling* — Continues to be largely prephonemic or early phonemic — initial consonants begin to appear as representing words and are sometimes strung together in sentences as ISTBFL (I see the butterfly)

# The Five Year Old: Curriculum

| | |
|---|---|
| **Writing** | • *Writing Themes* — Family; family trips; fairy tales; tales of good and evil; stories about pets; stories about themselves and best friends |
| | • *Handwriting* — Pencil grasp moves to a three fingered approach and letter formation tends to be all upper case; irregular spacing between words is related to beginning understanding of spelling |

| | |
|---|---|
| **Thematic Units** *(Social Studies, Science, Current Events)* | • Families; all about me, my body; babies; pets; our school; seasonal themes in nature (snow, winter, hibernation) |

| | |
|---|---|
| **Mathematics** | • Counting and sorting; set making; simple addition and subtraction using real materials; graphing |
| | • Beginning pencil and paper experiences with numbers |
| | • Practice with number formation |
| | • Simple equations |
| | • Continued exploration of size, shape, length, volume, as at four |

# Six Year Olds

*"But now I am six, I'm clever as clever.*
*So I think I'll be six for ever and ever."*

Now We Are Six
*by A.A. Milne*

One of my favorite children's books about school is by
Miriam Cohen with pictures by Lillian Hoban (illustrator of
*Bread and Jam for Francis*). The book is called *First Grade Takes
a Test* and in it the children are confounded by the experience
of taking a timed test for the first time. They have to keep still,
answer questions without help from their friends and finish
within a specified period of time. There are several hilarious
examples of six year old thinking which show that sixes are
not at all ready for formal testing. In my favorite:

"On the test there was a picture of Sally and Tom. Sally
was giving Tom something. It looked like a baloney
sandwich. Underneath it said:
   ☐ Sally is taller than Tom.
   ☐ Tom is taller than Sally.
Jim wondered what being tall had to do with getting

a baloney sandwich. And was it really a baloney sandwich? It might be tomato . . . Jim took a long time on that one."

Six is an age of dramatic physical, cognitive and social change. Tooth eruption is continuous; teachers find chewed pencils, papers and workbook corners in the first grade. Visual development is maturing, allowing for easy introduction of beginning reading tasks. Rapid physical growth is mirrored in rapid physical activity. Children are constantly in a hurry, rushing to be finished. They love to do their assignments, but are decidedly more interested in the process than in the product. Schoolwork tends to be sloppy or erratic. There is great interest in being first, in doing the most work, or in the opposite extreme. Children who can't be first may gladly be last; dawdling can be a favorite pastime. Along with great bursts of energy go periods of fatigue and frequent illnesses.

The importance of friends now rivals the importance of parents and teachers in the child's social development. Classrooms full of six year olds are busy, noisy places. Talking, humming, whistling, bustling are the order of the day.

"Industrious" describes the overall behavior of the child at six. S/he is now as interested in school work as spontaneous play. Children delight in cooperative projects, activities and tasks. No job is too big, no mountain too high. However, their eyes can be bigger than their stomachs or skills, and sixes risk an overpowering sense of inadequacy and inferiority as they tackle new frontiers. Teachers and parents need to remember that, at this age, the process is more important than the product.

The child is ordering and structuring the world in new ways. An ounce of encouragement for the six year old produces a radiant smile, hugs and excitement. An ounce of condemnation can produce tears, pouting and withdrawal. A teacher's words, tone, and body language all have a great effect on six year olds.

CHERRY WYMAN

It is at six that most children begin a major transition in their intellectual growth. The child now begins to approach the world more logically. Concepts begin to be organized in a symbolic manner through understandable systems and approaches. When they are younger, children are unable to accommodate an adult view of reality and generally don't understand adult explanations of cause and effect (although they may be accepted without challenge).

The beginning of reasoning is marked by the child's ability to identify differences, compensate for these differences and reverse an idea through mental activity. In one classic example of Piaget's, two equal balls of clay will be seen as equal quantities even after one is rolled out into a clay "snake" and compared to the ball by the six year old. Younger children, able to hold onto only one idea at a time, will see the "snake" as containing more clay because it is longer.

The difference between the five and six year old can be striking. The shift in cognitive development is accompanied by a shift in reasoning, an understanding of cause and effect in the natural world (e.g. what makes the clouds move) and a widening vision. Sixes can begin to see another's point of view and consider rules and conduct with greater objectivity.

In many ways this is a key moment, a turning point, an open door. At six, the child is extremely open, receptive to all new learning. The eagerness, curiosity, imagination, drive and enthusiasm of the six year old is perhaps never again matched in quantity or intensity during the life span.

# The Six Year Old: Growth Patterns

**Physical**
- Good visual pursuit for reading
- More aware of fingers as tools
- Sloppy; in a hurry; speed is a benchmark of 6
- Noisy in classroom
- Falls backwards out of chairs
- Learning to distinguish left from right
- Oral activity (teething) — chews pencils, fingernails, hair
- Easily tires; frequent illnesses
- Enjoys out of doors, gym

**Social**
- Wants to be first
- Competitive; enthusiastic
- Sometimes a "poor sport" or dishonest; invents rules
- Anxious to do well, but does a lot of testing
- Any failure is hard; thrives on encouragement
- Tremendous capacity for enjoyment; likes surprises, treats
- Can be bossy, teasing, critical of others
- Easily upset when hurt
- Friends are important (may have a best friend)
- School replaces home as most significant environmental influence

# The Six Year Old: Growth Patterns

**Language**
- Likes to "work"
- Likes to explain things; show & tell is useful
- Loves jokes & guessing games
- Boisterous & enthusiastic language
- Complainer

**Cognitive**
- Loves to ask questions
- Likes new games; ideas
- Loves to color; paint
- Learns best through discovery
- Enjoys process more than product
- Tries more than can accomplish (eyes bigger than stomach)
- Dramatic play elaborated
- Cooperative play elaborated
- Representative symbols more important
- Spatial relationships & functional relationships better understood
- Beginning understanding of past when tied closely to present
- Beginning interest in skill & technique for its own sake

# The Six Year Old in the Classroom
### First Grade or beginning Second

**Vision and Fine Motor Ability**

- Should do little copy work from blackboard; will comply if asked, but a difficult task
- Spacing and ability to stay on the line are difficult, inconsistent
- Tracking ability now makes reading instruction manageable

**Gross Motor Ability**

- Allow a busy level of noise and activity; children often work standing
- Encourage a slower pace or limit work to enhance quality

**Cognitive Growth**

- Games of all sorts are popular and useful — games, poems, riddles, and songs delight and illuminate; teaching through games produces stronger learning patterns than workbook learning
- Artistic explosion — clay, paints, dancing, coloring, book making, weaving, singing tried out seriously for first time; children need to feel their attempts are valued, that there is no right and wrong way to approach an art medium; risk-taking now enhances later artistic expression & competence

# The Six Year Old in the Classroom
### First Grade or beginning Second

| | |
|---|---|
| **Cognitive Growth** | • Expect high volume of products but low quality of completion — children are proud of how much they get done, but not concerned with looks |
| | • Pay attention to children's delight in the doing (especially for themselves) — includes academics, clean-up or snack; ready for experiments with individual and group responsibility |
| | • Social Studies content must be connected to here and now; field trips immensely popular, productive when followed by representational activities such as experience stories, work in blocks; children can only begin to understand past events (history) when closely associated with present |
| **Social Behavior** | • Extreme behavior needs to be understood but not excessively tolerated; tantrums, teasing, bossing, complaining, tattling are ways sixes try out relationships with authority |
| | • Extremely sensitive — an ounce of encouragement may be all a child needs to get over a difficult situation, severe criticism can truly injure |
| | • Take the competitive edge off games when used for learning; sixes are highly competitive and can overdo the need to win and be first |

# The Six Year Old: Curriculum

**Reading**
- Partner reading should continue
- Phonics instruction through whole language experiences with the whole class and small heterogeneous groups
- Introduction to the school or town library (may begin in kindergarten)
- "Predictable" books are still important, but also "easy" chapter books
- Simple expressive assignments about reading comprehension begin (writing, drawing, clay, painting, drama, blocks, construction)

**Writing**
- *Writing* — Drawing continues to have a big influence on story development; children form stories from a collection of drawings; begin to create with whole sentences, even if these sentences are early phonemic or use "letter name" spelling strategies — I WNT TO HR HS (I went to her house)
- *Spelling* — Letter naming (I lik to et candee — I like to eat candy) and "transitional" spelling (My frends ride bickes) predominate at this age; growing sense of phonetic clues is emerging and should be taught extensively

# The Six Year Old: Curriculum

**Writing**
- *Writing Themes* — Best friends; school-related stories; pets; going on trips; new possessions; holidays; fantasy
- *Handwriting* — Proper pencil grip; size of letters larger than at five and sloppier because writer is usually in a hurry or experimenting with new letter formation; upper and lower case used together spontaneously; spacing is unpredictable

**Thematic Units (Social Studies, Science, Current Events)**
- Families; friends; our school; workers in our school; themes in nature (butterflies, seasons, plants); jobs people do; differences (cultural, racial, language)

**Mathematics**
- Mental mathematics and problem solving begin *after* mastery of skill with concrete material
- Basic computation with money
- Simple worksheets to practice simple computation
- Experimentation with reversing operations (+ and -)
- Lots of experience with measuring (sand table, water table, outdoors, feet, blocks, etc.)
- Work with manipulatives must continue

# Seven Year Olds

*"On a bicycle I traveled over the known world's edge,*
*and the ground held. I was seven."*

An American Childhood
*by Annie Dillard*

An Upper Primary teacher at the Greenfield Center School, Bob Strachota, has devised a way to teach soccer to seven year olds that shows a clear understanding of the age and a streak of genius. The field is divided into three equal sections — a midfield and two goal zones. The class of 20–22 youngsters is first divided in half to make two teams and then each team is divided into thirds, with a third from each team placed in one of three sections of the field. Thus, three to four players on each team are restricted to their third of the field. The play is fast and furious in each section, but as soon as the ball passes over a section line, the players in that section must only watch as play is passed on to the next section.

This restriction of play responds, almost poetically, to the inclination of the seven for restriction, a direction governed by self-absorption and self-consciousness. "Sevens soccer" at the Center School has allowed all sevens to experience a measure of success on the playing field. Without these clear boundaries, many would have chosen to avoid the risk or withdraw all together. The others would dominate the field and show off for anyone watching.

In fact, sevens can be extremely moody, sulking and sometimes depressed. They are often content to spend long periods in their rooms, alone by choice, reading or listening to music or playing with animals or dolls. At school, too, they like to work by themselves and appreciate quiet corners for reading or working. They also like working with a best friend, although relationships may be on one day and off the next.

This is an inward, consolidating period of growth. Visually children exhibit myopic tendencies and concentrate on the details in their visual field. Their tiny printing is anchored to the baseline of the paper, their finger grip down on the lead of the pencil, their heads down on their arms or desk as they write, sometimes with one eye closed. Because of their visual concentration, sevens have great difficulty copying from the board and this task should be minimized. They do have a good working concept of right and left and general directionality.

Sevens are hard workers and often perfectionists. Where sixes are fond of the pencil sharpener, sevens adore the eraser. If they make mistakes they will erase and erase, sometimes putting a hole right through the paper. They want to be correct and they want their work to look good, too. Because of this tendency, they take a long time with everything they do and get very upset when they aren't given enough time to finish their work. Timed tests can be extremely upsetting.

If you schedule a class of seven year olds to take a spelling test at the end of the week, requesting that they spell the words correctly in their best handwriting, you are almost guaranteeing failure. They are capable of their best work in spelling *OR* in handwriting, but not both at the same time.

Sevens love the routine and structure of school and appreciate their personal relationship with the teacher. Substitute teachers often feel frustrated with sevens because they are constantly being told "That's not the way Teacher does it!"

In the classroom, sevens are good listeners and still enjoy being read a story. They show great interest in new words, number relationships and codes. They like working and talking with one other person (in board and card games, on puzzles) but don't always do well on group projects.

At six, children are noisy, verbal, active and brash; at seven, quieter, specific, passive, and sometimes tense. Sevens' industriousness is now concentrated on individual work. They hone in on what they can do and practice it over and over. If someone copies their work, the seven year old can become extremely upset. Music lessons, often introduced at this age, can be both rewarding and frustrating.

"I quit!" is often heard at home and on the playground, but it's not because they don't get their own way, although that's a frequent interpretation. They may walk away from a group game or a family project because of an overwhelming feeling of inferiority. Sevens' feelings need to be protected. Teasing, joking and especially sarcasm is painful to the seven year old. Being laughed at for a wrong answer or a "silly" idea can produce anger and tears.

At six, a child might respond to these feelings with a punch. Seven year olds are more apt to drive these feelings deep inside, and are less apt to risk themselves the next time they are called on or asked to do something. They are hypersensitive to physical ailments as well, both real and imagined.

Seven is an age where children are driven by curiosity and a strong internal desire to discover and invent. As they consolidate logical thinking, they begin to organize their internal mental structures in new ways. Now they can classify spontaneously: "Black bear, brown bear, grizzly bear, koala bear," they chant excitedly. They are intensely interested in how things work and love to take things apart and put them back together again, if they can. Working in a block corner holds as much fascination for the seven as for children at younger ages. Interlocking blocks and other small manipulatives are favorites and sevens delight in making miniature accessories for their block structures or social studies dioramas.

Sevens are beginning to deal with concepts of time, space and quantity with increased sophistication. While they must still act directly on their environment for understanding, they are increasingly able to represent their understanding symbolically in writing and drawing. Writing can be a favorite activity when children are given extended periods to create their own stories and narratives.

Science and social studies take on new meaning as sevens show increasing interest in the world around them. This interest will continue to expand and differentiate through ages eight, nine and ten. Study and understand the child's city or town before using textbooks to examine desert or mountain villages in foreign countries!

The child's increasing ability to do math without manipulatives, to infer, predict and estimate makes mathematical concepts particularly accessible at this age.

Seven is an age of intensity. Individualized activity consolidates new internal structures and feelings. A balance between hard work and self-assessment produces a sense of competence, setting the stage for greater self-direction at older ages.

# The Seven Year Old: Growth Patterns

**Physical**
- Visually myopic
- Works with head down on desk
- Pincer grasp at pencil point
- Written work tidy, neat
- Sometimes tense
- Likes confined space
- Many hurts, real and imagined

**Social**
- Inwardized, withdrawn
- Sometimes moody; depressed; sulking or shy
- Touchy
- "Nobody likes me"
- Changeable feelings
- Needs security, structure
- Relies on teacher for help
- Doesn't like to make mistakes or risk making them
- Sensitive to others' feelings, but sometimes tattles
- Conscientious; serious
- Keeps a neater desk, room
- Needs constant reinforcement
- Strong likes and dislikes

# The Seven Year Old: Growth Patterns

**Language**
- Good listener
- Precise talker
- Likes one-to-one conversation
- Vocabulary development expands rapidly
- Interested in meaning of words
- Likes to send notes
- Interested in all sorts of codes

**Cognitive**
- Likes to review learning
- Needs closure; must complete assignments
- Likes to work slowly
- Likes to work alone
- Can classify spontaneously
- Likes to be read to
- Reflective ability growing
- Erases constantly, wants work perfect
- Likes to repeat tasks
- Likes board games
- Enjoys manipulatives
- Wants to discover how things work; likes to take things apart

# The Seven Year Old in the Classroom

**Vision and Fine Motor Ability**

- Printing, drawing, number work tend to be small, if not microscopic; work with head down on desk, often hiding or closing one eye
- Copying from the board can be harmful
- Not the time to introduce cursive handwriting
- Printing and drawing anchored to bottom line; difficult to fill up space
- Often work with 3-fingered grasp at pencil point and find it difficult to relax grip

**Gross Motor Ability**

- Plan for quieter room; sustained, quiet work periods with little overflow behavior
- Prefer board games to gym games; playground games (jump rope, 4 square, hopscotch) become more popular than team or large group activities

# The Seven Year Old in the Classroom

**Cognitive Growth**

- Pay special attention to routine and need for closure — want to finish work they begin, need a warning to prepare for transitions; timed tests can be especially troublesome

- Like to work by themselves or in two's; memorization popular along with codes, puzzles and other secrets

- Want their work to be perfect; classroom attention to products, proper display of work is entirely appropriate

- Enjoy repeating tasks, reviewing assignments verbally with teacher; like to touch base frequently with teacher

- "Discovery" centers or projects often successful; like to collect and sort

**Social Behavior**

- Frequent friendship shifts; work best in pairs alone; accept teacher seating assignments

- Schedule changes upsetting; plan well for substitutes

- Moderate seriousness of classroom with humor and games

- Communication with parents often critical during this changeable age

- Anxiety about tests, assignments, recess can produce physical complaints

# The Seven Year Old: Curriculum

**Reading**
- "Silent reading" is not yet silent — lots of whispering (vocalizing) as children read
- Individual reading becomes stronger than partner reading
- Phonics instruction intensifies through small reading group instruction
- Formal spelling program introduced (also as part of writing)
- Reading comprehension assignments continue and include more written responses

**Writing**
- *Writing* — Longer stories with beginning, middle and end emerge; sometimes "chapter" books; the story line is all important; everything from "breakfast to bed"; now writing comes before drawing and sometimes does not even include drawing
- *Spelling* — Correct spelling slowly emerges from transitional with increased phonetic and sight word fluency; a formal spelling program appropriately begins; "invented" spelling should still be accepted because revision is still not seen as necessary or important; capitalization and punctuation easily taught

# The Seven Year Old: Curriculum

**Writing**

- *Writing Themes* — Family; friends; sleeping over; losing teeth (also at six); trips; pets (often including first stories about death of pets); death of family members; illness; war; famine; or other serious issues; nightmares; nonfiction writing can be introduced as a way to show learning from concrete science or social studies investigation

- *Handwriting* — Pencil grip down on shaft of pencil, often right on the lead; a very tight grip, often over-tense; size of letters is often microscopic, anchored to the baseline; *not* a good age to introduce cursive handwriting — introduce it to younger or older children

# The Seven Year Old: Curriculum

**Thematic Units** *(Social Studies, Science, Current Events)*
- Our neighborhood; how systems work (plumbing, lighting, heating in our school; how we get our milk; how the cafeteria works); jobs people do; things we are good at; cultural and racial diversity, discrimination; natural science themes (pond, forest, meadow)

**Mathematics**
- Increased computation with money
- Time
- More complex mental mathematics; equation solving
- Fractions through measurement, weighing, comparing
- Symmetry and other simple geometry (unit blocks, pattern blocks)
- Simple computation with multiplication, division based on experience with concrete materials
- Continued use of games as vehicle for skill practice

# Eight Year Olds

*"Mothers for miles around worried about Zuckerman's swing. They feared some child would fall off. But no child ever did. Children almost always hang onto things tighter than their parents think they will."*

Charlotte's Web
*by E.B. White*

"Teacher, we have a great idea!"

Watch out! Here come the eight year olds — full of energy, imagination and little sense of their own limits.

"We have this great idea to do a play about Rosa Parks and we have all the clothes at home and we're going to bring them in tomorrow and we can use your desk for the bus, and we can make tickets and charge admission and we'll put it on tomorrow . . . OK?"

There's no thought of a script, assigning parts, rehearsal schedules, the hard work of learning lines, practice, costumes, set, and finally production. It's all a blur of enthusiasm tempered by only a vague understanding of how things get done.

The job of the second or third grade teacher is to harness that energy and give it some direction and focus. Teachers need to help children cut work down to bite-size pieces throughout the year. This includes homework assignments, which should never be longer than a half-hour in duration and should be limited in scope and expectations. Children at this age need to experience "incremental success" in their school work — success in gradually increasing quantities and levels of complexity — so they will continue to be motivated and excited.

Eight year olds tend to gravitate toward their own gender when making choices about working and playing with others. On the playground, the waves of boys chasing girls or girls chasing boys at recess are often eight year olds. Boys especially tend to be fascinated by the world of "smutty" jokes at this age, but both boys and girls enjoy virtually any kind of humor, including riddles, limericks, and knock-knock jokes.

A key developmental struggle is gaining competence over the tools of their trade. At school, this means industrious efforts in such areas as handwriting, handcrafts, computer skills, drawing and sketching, and simple geometry. But when accomplishments don't come easily or quickly, there is a strong sense of inferiority. Patience is not common in eight year olds. Again, assignments in handwriting or spelling, for instance, need to be short and to the point. Drafts of children's work as well as beautiful, finished work should be liberally displayed in the classroom so that children can see the range of effort required to make progress toward mastery in a certain area. Children also benefit by graphing or charting their progress in certain areas so that the teacher can combat that feeling of "I'll never get this . . . I'll never be able to do this."

"I'm bored!" is a common complaint of the eight year old. Adult translation: This is too hard! Look beyond these words to what they are showing you in their work. Redirection and encouragement go a long way; criticism can be devastating.

Often, parents and teachers lament about an eight year old, "He could do it if he only tried. He's lazy and unmotivated. He never sticks to any one thing for more than a day." The eight year old is actually exploring his potential. He is struggling with feelings of inferiority as he tries out one new area after another in an expanding awareness of the broader world. This uncertainty will hit a peak at nine.

# The Eight Year Old: Growth Patterns

**Physical**
- Speedy, works in a hurry
- Full of energy
- Needs physical release, outdoor time
- Somewhat awkward
- Attention span limited
- Vision strong in near and far

**Social**
- Gregarious, humorous
- Likes to work cooperatively
- Often "bites off more than can chew"; overestimates abilities
- Resilient; bounces back quickly from mistakes
- Prefers same gender activities
- Trouble with limits and boundaries
- Friendship groups often include more children than at seven

# The Eight Year Old: Growth Patterns

**Language**
- Talkative
- Listens, but so full of ideas cannot always recall what has been said
- Exaggerates
- Likes to explain ideas
- Vocabulary expands rapidly

**Cognitive**
- Engrossed in activity at hand; loves to socialize at same time
- Likes groups and group activity
- Very industrious
- Often works quickly
- Concrete operations solidifying
- Basic skills begin to be mastered
- Begins to feel a sense of competence with skills

# The Eight Year Old in the Classroom

**Vision and Fine Motor Ability**

- Acuity and control come together; appropriate time to focus on cursive handwriting — children love to practice, but product often sloppy

- Pencil grasp should now be "adult"; if not, a "pencil grip" may still be needed to help correct habits

- Can copy from board and handle increasingly complex (but not lengthy) assignments

**Gross Motor Ability**

- Often a "growth spurt" — restless and need lots of physical activity; short exercise breaks (even in the classroom) help concentration

- Love group games on the playground; gravitate toward same gender activities, so teacher should lead outdoor games for whole class (tag games, etc.)

- Play hard and often exhaust themselves in short time; several short play breaks more productive than one long one

**Cognitive Growth**

- Very industrious, but often exaggerate ability, have trouble knowing limits; teachers can shorten (rather than lengthen) assignments; success in small doses builds confidence

# The Eight Year Old in the Classroom

| | |
|---|---|
| **Cognitive Growth** | • Love to work cooperatively, most productive in groups; enjoys responsibility — though not always successful |
| | • Interest in process and product of school work; peers' assessment of work as important as teacher's |
| | • Work usually well organized, though tends to be sloppy; need teacher assistance with organizational strategies, especially on tasks such as math papers copied from textbooks |
| | • Growing interest in rules, logic; keen interest in how things are put together, how they work; interest in natural world and classification |
| | • Tire easily, may give up temporarily on hard assignments, but bounce back quickly |
| **Social Behavior** | • Classroom organization should feature desks in groups, or groups at tables; teacher should change groupings frequently through the year |
| | • Respond to class projects and traditions which build a sense of unity and cohesion |
| | • Gender issues become more important |
| | • Fairness issues, growing sense of moral responsibility beyond self; arguing |
| | • Respond to studies of other cultures, stories that concern fairness, justice |

# The Eight Year Old: Curriculum

**Reading**
- Reading groups based on trade books organized heterogeneously around interests of children within reachable skill range
- Independent reading program introduced with simple independent assignments or projects (such as book covers, interviews, dioramas) designed to spur class interest in reading and show reading comprehension
- Lengthier chapter books with more advanced themes introduced for read-aloud time

**Writing**
- *Writing* — Quite lengthy stories with increasingly descriptive language; interest in diverse writing genres such as poetry, newspaper articles, cartoons; the "breakfast to bed" story-line is a favorite, providing more detail than any reader (except the author) would care to know about; beginnings of draft and revision are meaningful
- *Spelling* — Correct spelling improves; compound words taught; use of dictionary, alphabetical order; phonetic mistake patterns more noticeable and students with real difficulty in spelling easier to spot; practice with capitalization and punctuation continues

# The Eight Year Old: Curriculum

**Writing**
- *Writing Themes* — Adventure and "breakfast to bed" stories; sports with friends and heroes; horses, unicorns and other mythical beasts; stories based on cartoons; "chapter" books; poetry about nature, the seasons; use of nonfiction writing like at seven continues

- *Handwriting* — Good posture, pencil grip and fluid movement of arm and hand across page; excellent time to introduce cursive handwriting and provide lots of time for practice; children enjoy this practice and want to become competent, though easily frustrated.

**Thematic Units**
*(Social Studies, Science, Current Events)*
- Our neighborhood; our community (interdependence); community institutions (bank, newspaper, radio); long ago *OR* far away (but not both); themes in nature (trees, rocks, animals); cultural and racial diversity; beginning history

# The Eight Year Old: Curriculum

**Mathematics** • All four operations used in problem solving
   • Fractions through measurement, weighing, and some pencil and paper tasks
   • Borrowing and carrying
   • Geometric patterns constructed with pencil and paper
   • Games provide arena to practice strategy

# Nine Year Olds

*"My ninth year was certainly more exciting than any of the others.
But not all of it was exactly what you would call fun."*

Danny the Champion of the World
*by Roald Dahl*

"I hate living in Greenfield! It is so boring! It isn't a city town.
It isn't a country town either. It isn't a suburb town and it isn't
the kind of town you'd visit your Aunt Mabel in. It is a medium
sized town with a few country back roads, a few corner stores,
a few movie theaters, some restaurants and many houses. It
doesn't sound too bad you say? It is. The trouble is there's
nothing to do! The most exciting thing that's ever happened
to me in Greenfield was a train derailment. And it turned out
o.k. You see, if you go to Boston you have the swan boats, you
go to California, you have the beach, you go to Greenfield you
have . . . . um-um . . . see what I mean. That's why I wish
Greenfield were better." (Thanks to Kate Arsenault — now a
young adult!)

I've never forgotten this essay with its exclamation marks
and sardonic humor as a benchmark of the often confused and

## Nine

troubled age of nine. The enthusiasm of eight often turns into dark brooding and worrying at nine — worrying about world events, about the health of parents, about moving away, about losing best friends, about changing schools. Teachers engaged in "writing process" note these thinly veiled themes again and again in fiction writing.

Sometimes the deep seriousness of these social concerns can bring a twinkle to the adult eye. One nine year old worked diligently on her protest poster on a Saturday morning: "Save the Elephants — Ban Ivory Soap."

Nines complain about their aches and pains, their cuts and bruises and their hurt feelings. Nail biting, hair twisting and other outlets for tension are common. Test taking can be a disaster, and it's easy to hypothesize about the well-known dip in fourth grade test scores and the anxiousness of nines. The best test takers are the risk takers in the world; nines are anything but good risk takers.

Teachers at this level see children finish their tests early simply because they put down any answer, rather than think through what they know. Others get only halfway through because they get stuck trying to figure out one right answer, refusing to be wrong. Nines need many opportunities to practice test-taking before the real thing — modelling and role-playing can defuse the anxiety created by tests.

Compared to younger and older schoolmates, nines tend to learn better on their own as they gain mastery of basic skills. They're gaining a more solid understanding of key cognitive concepts such as multiplication, spelling patterns, and scientific process. Younger children enjoy experimenting with these processes, but nines now take care with the final product. They will work hard on a science report on butterflies, study for weekly spelling tests or a chapter test in math.

Nothing is fair to the nine year old, who is also struggling with the cognitive task of understanding ethical behavior at a new level. Many nines feel they are singled out for unfair treatment by a teacher, parent or Little League coach. This is also a way children relate to a growing sense of peer importance and group solidarity: "You're never fair to *us* . . . *we* never get to do anything." And there is a growing sense that nothing is fair in the world. Why do children die? Why is there AIDS? Why are there poor people and how come a few people have all the money?

Teachers of nine year olds in third and fourth grade need a sense of humor and a determined lightness to challenge the sometimes deadly seriousness of the age. Their growing peer solidarity can be channeled into wonderful club activities — i.e., stamps, chess, rocks. Positive language is also essential for children's growth. An ounce of negative criticism is greatly magnified by the nine year old. An ounce of encouragement is as well.

# The Nine Year Old: Growth Patterns

**Physical**
- Increased coordination
- Pushes self to physical limits
- Fatigues easily
- Numerous injuries
- Somatic complaints
- Tension outlets such as nail-biting, hair-twisting, lip-pursing

**Social**
- Highly competitive
- Self-aware
- Impatient
- Worrier; anxious
- Aloof
- Complainer; fairness issues
- Sees adult inconsistencies and imperfections
- Critical
- Can be sullen and moody
- Individualistic

# The Nine Year Old: Growth Patterns

**Language**
- Descriptive
- Loves vocabulary and language play and information
- Baby-talk sometimes re-emerges
- Use of hyperbole
- Age of negatives: "I hate it," "I can't," "boring," "yeah, right"
- "Dirty" jokes
- Graffiti

**Cognitive**
- Industrious and self-critical
- Dawn of "bigger world"
- Less imaginative
- Intellectual curiosity
- Ability to deal with multiple variables emerges
- Trouble with abstractions — large numbers, periods of time or space

# The Nine Year Old in the Classroom

| | |
|---|---|
| **Vision and Fine Motor Abilities** | • Increased coordination leads to greater control, interest in detail; cursive handwriting can be fully mastered; watch for overly tight pencil grip |
| | • Practice with a variety of fine motor tools and tasks useful (weaving, knitting, carving, drawing) |
| | • Can copy from board, recopy assignments, produce beautiful "final drafts" |
| **Gross Motor Ability** | • Push to the limit — love to challenge themselves individually, race against each other or against clock |
| | • Physical control an issue; knowing boundaries and staying within them a physical and social issue |
| | • Boys love to rough-house — "puppy stage" |
| | • Age of physical complaints, frequent injuries — some real, some exaggerated |
| | • Gym class a challenge — can't sit still |
| **Cognitive Growth** | • Can work in groups; arguing, disputes about facts, rules, directions may take longer than actual activity |
| | • Homework should be reasonable, related specifically to next day's work; asks, "Why do we have to do this?" |

# The Nine Year Old in the Classroom

| | |
|---|---|
| **Cognitive Growth** | • Looking hard (often anxious) for explanation of facts, how things work, why things happen as they do; good age for scientific exploration |
| | • Reading to learn, instead of learning to read |
| | • Takes pride in finished work, attention to detail; enjoys the product, but may jump quickly between interests |
| **Social Behavior** | • Likes to work with partner of choice — usually same gender; cliques may begin |
| | • Fairness issues increase; can be deadly serious about competitiveness — competition in the curriculum, gym classes, etc. should be presented with a sense of fun, lightness, humor |
| | • Likes to negotiate — age of "Let's make a deal" |
| | • Worries (school work, the world) need teacher patience and understanding; clear language when giving directions, setting expectations very important; *avoid sarcastic humor*, children are their own worst critics |
| | • Second chances important, tendency to give up; encourage and build up fragile sense of ability to accomplish tasks |
| | • Exasperation by teacher or whining voice leads to more complaints, whining, moodiness; laughing with nines is the best medicine |

# The Nine Year Old: Curriculum

**Reading**
- Reading Groups continue; assignments involve beginning research tasks, use of related reading material
- Dictionary skills taught intensively (although introduced at earlier ages)
- Some children may volunteer to read orally during read-aloud
- Major poetry unit or poetry throughout the year begins in earnest (although introduced at earlier ages)

**Writing**
- *Writing* — Emphasis can be placed on first draft and revision process; descriptive writing can be taught more deliberately as well as character development, plot, cohesiveness and believability
- *Spelling* — Use of dictionary improves as does first draft spelling; functional spelling as in journals, other subject writing shows increasingly fewer mistakes; weekly testing appropriate; basic capitalization and punctuation usually mastered
- *Writing Themes* — Moving away, divorce, death, disease, and other worries predominate; world issues; non-fiction writing; poetry about feelings, darker themes.; "writer's block" common

# The Nine Year Old: Curriculum

**Writing**
- *Handwriting* — Increasingly fluent in cursive; begin to use in day-to-day assignments and in spontaneous writing; much neater than at eight.

**Thematic Units**
*(Social Studies, Science, Current Events)*
- Our country and world; long ago and far away; history of culture (Egypt, Africa); racial and ethnic diversity; environmental concerns in the immediate environment (trash, air or water pollution); literature characters or a theme focused around a particular book

**Mathematics**
- Division
- Extensive experience with word problems
- Computation with money, introduction of decimals
- Practice with multiplication tables

# Ten Year Olds

*"Mrs. Hanson told Diane and me to get our folders and place them on our desks. I made a pretty semicircle with mine. I was glad I had only good papers for my parents to see."*

Nothing's Fair in Fifth Grade
*by Barthe DeClements*

"Can we stay in today and finish the book? Please!"

"Will you read more of the story this afternoon, Mrs. Goodwin? We promise to do our math for homework if you would. The story is so awesome!"

"Yeah," comes the chorus of hushed voices.

"Well . . . all right, children . . . but just one more chapter," yields Mrs. Goodwin, silently delighting in one of those magic moments of teaching, one she will always treasure about this class.

The children settle back in, sprawling on the carpet, or chins on hands at their desks; two girls lean against Mrs. Goodwin as she reads from her comfy chair. The story continues.

These scenes are repeated often at age ten. To exaggerate a little . . . here is the golden end of childhood. At ten, children find comfort in themselves, their teachers, their parents, and even their siblings! They relax in their childhood, gathering strength for the impending storm of adolescence and consolidating their gains from early childhood. You can see this clearly in the cognitive choices that children make in school. Tens concentrate, even relish, working on tangible products that display their competence — book reports, theme reports, beginning research writing, scientific documentation.

These industrious children are also able to easily share their knowledge with their classmates and work well on group projects. This is the ideal age for the class play or trip, and tens can often help elevens and even twelves in cooperative pursuits because of their relative calm and instinct for cooperation.

At ten, children seem to be the most "actively receptive" as learners of factual information. This is usually a good time to master the multiplication tables that have been such a struggle until now. It's an age for state capitals, presidents, principle products of major nations, exports and imports, poetry and speech memorization. Education about the human body, sex, childbirth and child rearing (as determined by the school's curriculum policy) can be more effective now than a year or two later when children are more self-conscious about their bodies. The "facts" are more easily taught and remembered, and boys and girls work well together.

Children know all the rules at ten thanks to their facile memories. Board games and games of strategy are great favorites and there tends to be mutual agreement rather than endless arguing about rules. It's a wonderful age to teach or reteach mediation to children, to introduce or reintroduce problem-solving formats in class meeting, to teach governmental structures and scientific principles. All these will be challenged at eleven, argued with at twelve and rebelled against at thirteen. But ten is a great time for initial introduction and general acceptance, to plant the seeds for the more formal and more abstract cognitive challenges ahead.

Outdoor play is as critical for preadolescent children as it is for children in early childhood (See "Exercise" section in the Developmental Issues Affecting All Children, p. 17). Schools

MARLYNN CLAYTON

that have eliminated recess have taken away the inalienable right and undeniable need of children to play. Breaks are especially important to these industrious ten year olds and allow them to bounce back and do even more school work. Five minutes of jumping jacks, a run around the school building, "Head and Shoulders, Knees and Toes," elevates the blood and oxygen levels in the body and brain. (Try this in the middle of standardized testing! You'll see positive results.)

Tens especially love group games outdoors and can be taught and enjoy cooperative and non-competitive activities as well as more traditional and competitive games like kickball, tag and dodgeball. Boys and girls play well together in either kind of activity. Group initiatives and challenges have great success at this age, so it is a good time for formal outdoor education like a "ropes course" challenge or overnight camping. Children often have their fondest memories of weeks at summer camp at ten.

Ordering their world is central to the ten year old. Enjoy the clean bedroom, the orderly classroom, and the relative absence of arguments. Observe and capitalize on children's interest in classification and seriation: rock collections, baseball and superhero cards, doll and teddy bear and unicorn collections, jewelry boxes, secret compartments. Teach about phylum and genus and other ways of organizing the world. Teach beginning genetics, the value of repeating experiments and testing variables. Teach about attributes and combinations of attributes to describe different phenomena. The world is theirs to organize.

# The Ten Year Old: Growth Patterns

**Physical**
- Large muscle development
- Desperately need outdoor time and physical challenge
- Handwriting often sloppier than at nine
- Snacks and rest periods helpful for growing bodies

**Social**
- Fairness issues peak and can be solved!
- Quick to anger — quick to forgive
- Generally content
- Work very well in groups
- Enjoy both family and peers
- Like clubs, activities, sports
- Usually truthful; developing more mature sense of right and wrong, good at solving social issues

# The Ten Year Old: Growth Patterns

**Language**
- Good listeners, actively receptive
- Voracious readers
- Expressive, talkative, like to explain
- Cooperative *and* competitive
- Friendly, generally happy

**Cognitive**
- Memorization productive
- Increased ability to abstract
- Likes rules and logic
- Classification and collections of interest; likes to organize
- Able to concentrate, read for extended periods
- Good problem solvers
- Proud of academic products

# The Ten Year Old in the Classroom

**Vision and Fine Motor Abilities**

- Able to focus well, concentrate on task at hand; integrate spelling, dictation, penmanship well, but precision may be lacking as many skills come into play at once

- Particularly enjoy tracing and copying as fine motor skills strengthen; maps, "cartooning" provide excellent fine motor practice

- Use of tools (compass, protractor, ruler, templates) can be introduced successfully; need plenty of practice time

**Gross Motor Ability**

- Need a great deal of physical activity, large muscle development; upper body strength generally undeveloped; extra recess, play time a must or will spill over into acting-out behavior

- Love group games, relays, group initiatives; class outings, "ropes courses," double-dutch clubs, team sports, other organized activities

**Cognitive Growth**

- Highly productive with school work; usually conscientious with homework; pay close attention to form, structure, directions, organization

# The Ten Year Old in the Classroom

**Cognitive Growth**

- Actively receptive learners; memorization a key teaching strategy; love geography, World Book of Records, facts about sports & TV, spelling, math, computer and electronic games; choral reading, singing, poetry, plays popular

- Classification, seriation, exactness are strengths — collections, science and math projects highly productive; height of concrete organizational skills

**Social Behavior**

- Basically cooperative nature encourages group activity, whole class cohesion, cooperative learning; good age to introduce and train for peer mediation, conflict resolution

- Friendship and fairness issues constantly being played out; use teams, groups, games, competition to allow for practice in social interaction

- Generally satisfied with own ability, happy and flexible; can be challenged by teacher to reach out to others; good age to start cross-age tutoring — love serving in role as teacher of younger children; also enjoy community service projects

- Enjoy being noticed, rewarded for efforts; "noticing" language an important teacher tool

- Quick tempers may lead to physical outbursts and tears, but usually quickly and easily solved

# The Ten Year Old: Curriculum

**Reading**
- Poetry captivating; love to memorize and recite; also choral readings and plays a great favorite
- Trade books centered around themes begin to entice readers (*Nothing's Fair in Fifth Grade*)
- Independent reading a favorite activity, children want to devour one book after another — allow a separate period for this activity without book project being required as often
- High interest in comic books

**Writing**
- *Writing* — Lengthy chapter books, longer poems, first research papers, writing about famous people — all usually filled with light and descriptive language; humor may emerge in writing more frequently; use of dialogue deepens as well as good interaction between characters
- *Spelling* — Enjoy memorizing spelling lists and are challenged positively by difficult words; ability to do well on tests and to spell well functionally do not always coincide

# The Ten Year Old: Curriculum

**Writing**
- *Writing Themes* — Friends, friends and more friends in many adventures; time travel; letter writing for information; note writing to friends; report writing
- *Handwriting* — Functionally fluent cursive or keyboarding for those having great difficulty

**Thematic Units**
**(Social Studies, Science, Current Events)**
- Geography; immigration; history; how things work; geology, land formations, weather; industry (research of a particular product to its source); games

**Mathematics**
- Multiplication tables mastered
- Decimals taught extensively
- Extensive computation with fractions
- Measurement, and measurement computation with maps
- Double-digit division

# Eleven Year Olds

*"Phillip nodded. `For a girl, you take jokes better than anybody.'
Suddenly he pointed down the road and this time the yellow bus
was really on its way. He smiled a dimpled smile and I remembered
why he's the cutest boy in the J.T. Williams School."*

Phillip Hall Likes Me I Reckon Maybe
*by Bette Greene*

It's near the end of the morning's math lesson and the children are growing fidgety. The teacher is on a roll; rapid-fire questions are answered correctly one after another:

"What's another name for a parallelogram? . . . Yes, Max?"

"It's past time for recess, teacher, we're missing our recess!"

A chorus of agreement greets the teacher.

Finally out at recess, the fifth and sixth graders mill around on the kickball field.

"Same teams as yesterday!" yells one girl.

"No way!" screams another, "You smushed us yesterday."

"Yeah, but Jamal isn't here today that makes it even," says the first girl.

"Yeah, but look who you got today," says the other. The arguments continue. Ten full minutes of their precious recess time is used making up teams. No one seems to mind.

As children move from ten to eleven, major changes begin to take place. In their cognitive growth, children seem to be challenging all their assumptions about the world and in turn they challenge many of the adult parameters they have previously accepted as relatively clear and just. Cognitive structures in the brain seem to be rearranging themselves with the same speed that the body is beginning to rearrange itself.

Eleven, of course, marks the beginning of adolescence, especially for girls, whose physical growth is generally way ahead of the boys. The onset of menstruation is common at eleven, the average being at twelve. As their bodies change, emotional sensitivity and volatility increase. The clear physical difference between boys and girls leads to natural separation between boys and girls in the classroom and on the playground.

While mixed-gender activity still happens and should certainly still be encouraged, it is not as spontaneously attractive for children as it was at ten. Watch how children come to the meeting circle or to a game, the boys on one side, the girls on another. Boys are watching the girls change and wondering when something is going to happen to them. Both genders are interested in knowledge about sex and changing bodies and this education should continue for both (as determined by the school's curriculum policy).

Elevens in fifth and sixth grade appear to be more absorbed in their own individual academic accomplishments in the classroom, and simultaneously more interested in their peers also. This creates uncertainty for teachers and students. Challenges begin through trial and error and soon teachers face challenges on nearly every subject — assignments; homework; rules in the classroom; interpretations of literature, history, and governmental policy; adult authority in general. These should be seen and addressed as signs of cognitive as well as social growth!

These challenges aren't always polite or on target, but elevens are engaged in significant changes in their learning approaches and strategies. Their awkwardness and sometimes apparent "rudeness" commonly causes conflict between parents and children as well as teachers and children if the developmental issues aren't understood. Elevens are often genuinely surprised that adults take offense at their challenges and are easily hurt. Parents and teachers also struggle because just a little while ago, at ten, the child was so easy to get along with, such a delightful and reasonable friend to have around.

"Saving face" is very important for the easily-embarrassed eleven year old, even in seemingly innocuous situations. It's especially important to try not to correct the eleven year old in front of his/her peers, but to find a time and place away from the group. When possible, finding a time that is removed from the incident itself is also helpful.

The growing cognitive strength of the eleven year old is fed by learning new and demanding skills in research, such as footnoting, bibliography, and scientific notation. It's also a good age for learning on the computer. They're especially turned off by traditional workbooks, ditto sheets, and other packaged programs that claim to teach "real life skills." Instead, they need the opportunity to interview the fire chief, take notes at a local meeting, or write a letter to a map company or local corporation.

APPLE LORD

While their new skills in these more adult realms may be crude and tentative at first, elevens are motivated by the opportunity to try out brand new arenas of knowledge. Foreign language, music and new forms of artistic expression are also attractive. These challenges aren't met without complaint. Easily frustrated, the eleven year old may fuss about how hard something is to their teacher, while telling their parents how cool the new subject is, or vice versa. For example, something as hard as written dictation can be outwardly hated but inwardly cherished as a delicious intellectual challenge.

Girls at eleven are at the height of forming cliques, which can result in a great deal of cruelty as well as wonderful friendship groups. Cliquish behavior seems to be a way for young girls to practice forming deep attachments that generally characterize older female relationships and which differentiate them from the more distant and less effusive relationships of both young boys and older males. While this, like much else about developmental patterns, is a generalization, it seems substantiated by much of the recent research by Carol Gilligan and others (Gilligan, 1982).

A teacher's role in dealing with cliques is a delicate balance between letting girls work things out for themselves and providing direct mediation. My experience is that if three girls can't solve a problem within a ten minute time limit, teacher intervention is necessary.

Sports and outdoor activity are important to elevens, but often include arguments about team effort and the interpretation of rules. Elevens also focus on their own personal skill development in a sport and are constantly comparing themselves to the best athletes. Some will drop out of competitive sports at this age (or at twelve) as competition gets increasingly serious and the skills more difficult. Teachers and coaches can encourage continued participation by focusing on effort rather than excellence. Trying hard is rewarded as much as scoring.

Changing bodies also affect the willingness of some girls to continue in individual activities such as dance, gymnastics or swimming. Boys struggle with awkwardness in athletics at this age (as well as at twelve and thirteen) as they begin to shoot up. For both boys and girls, muscles don't keep pace with bones, and aches and pains at night and complaints on the field and in the classroom are common.

The awkwardness of adolescence is just beginning, both physically and emotionally. Eleven signifies even more difficult, as well as joyous, years ahead. It's a time when both teachers and parents need to sharpen their skills in translating language, facial expression, moods and intentions. Mothers, for instance, often report that daughters are exceptionally critical and mean — "I can't seem to do anything right!" Feelings and relationships in adolescence are seldom clear and simple.

# The Eleven Year Old: Growth Patterns

**Physical**
- Vast appetite for food and physical activity and talking
- Growth spurt of early adolescence for some girls
- Constant motion; restless
- More illness: colds, flu, ear infections
- Need for more sleep
- Physical aggression not uncommon
- Fine motor capability good

**Social**
- Moody; sensitive
- Oppositional; tests limits
- Often does best away from home
- Impulsive; rude; unaware
- Loves to argue
- Difficulty with decisions
- Self-absorbed
- Extremes of emotion
- Inclusion/exclusion; height of cliques; seeks to belong

# The Eleven Year Old: Growth Patterns

**Language**
- Discovery of the telephone
- Impulsive — talks before thinking
- Can be cruel
- Argumentative; debater
- Appreciates humor
- Imitates adult language

**Cognitive**
- Prefers new tasks and experiences to reflection or revision of previous work
- Able to abstract
- Deductive reasoning advances
- Can establish and modify rules, develop hypotheses
- Increased ability to de-center and see world from various perspectives
- Loves to argue

# The Eleven Year Old in the Classroom

**Vision and Fine Motor Ability**

- Highly improved, more confident of skills; can explore delicate work (calligraphy, linoleum block printing, Japanese brush stroke); art an important vehicle to greater focus in reading, math

- May complain of headaches, only read for short periods of time; music (portable tapes, listening centers) may aid concentration

- Handwork (weaving, braiding, sewing) often a favorite; may aid concentration and serve as emotional outlet for stress

**Gross Motor Ability**

- Love challenge of competition; prefer team sports, improving ability to play as a team

- Individual motor skills (throwing, catching, kicking) accelerate rapidly; likes to measure individual best

- "Quiet time" in school day useful for physical rest, break from academics and social dynamics

**Cognitive Growth**

- Scientific study, mathematical problem solving, invention, debate accentuate new abilities in deductive reasoning; hands-on learning stilll critical for most

- Focus on self, imagining adult roles makes history, biography, current events exciting

# The Eleven Year Old in the Classroom

**Cognitive Growth**

- Interest in rules (and challenging rules) makes board games, intellectual puzzles, brain teasers, even tests enjoyable, productive
- Reasonably hard work usually challenges rather than defeats; need help with time-management skills, homework
- Learns well in cooperative groups
- Likes work that feels grown-up — research, bibliography, interviews, footnotes, math skills
- May show interest, facility in languages, music, mechanics; time to explore these areas important
- Intellectual interest in older & very young people

**Social Behavior**

- Desire to test limits, rules, an important developmental milestone, not personal attack on teacher; class meetings, peer mediation, student councils, cross-age tutoring highly effective
- Teacher attitude, tone, sense of humor critical; prevent them from taking themselves *too* seriously
- Inclusion/exclusion issues require changing structures to adjust social mix
- "Saving face" important; not necessary for teacher to "win" arguments; provide private, physical space to think things over

# The Eleven Year Old: Curriculum

**Reading**
- Week-long reading assignments begin, still utilizing trade books
- Increased use of non-fiction reading tied to subject area knowledge
- Biographies a favorite
- Enjoy reading to children in younger grades, especially helpful for less fluent readers

**Writing**
- *Writing* — Benefit greatly from the opportunity to rehearse their writing; plot, character, style, personal interest in varied subject matter all expand and begin to take on characteristics of "adult" writing; research report writing still very rudimentary and tied to source material; poetry writing a favorite as is cartooning; revision can be a struggle
- *Spelling* — Accurate or difficult depending on child; most enjoy challenge of difficult words; dictionary skills emphasized
- *Writing Themes* — Quite varied and individual for advanced writers; blood and gore, fantasy, science fiction, love and romance
- *Handwriting* — Functional for most

# The Eleven Year Old: Curriculum

**Thematic** • Games; history; biography; government;
**Units** community service; physical development,
*(Social Studies*, the body systems; plant growth and other
*Science*, forms of systematic measurement
*Current Events)*

**Mathematics** • Complicated word problems
• Probability and statistics through real problems
• Use of calculator and computer in mathematics
• Computation for speed and accuracy
• Percentage

# Twelve Year Olds

*"I am not a nut. I am a pioneer."*

The Real Me
*by Betty Miles*

The oldest excuse in the world — "The dog ate my homework" — has changed for the economic group of twelve year olds lucky enough to have computers at home.

"Mrs. Abernathy, the printer chewed up my paper."

"My dad was using the computer."

"My baby sister erased all my files."

But the excuses are just as inventive, with or without computers:

"I couldn't find any paper in the house."

"I left my book on the bus. Has anybody seen my book?"

"You didn't tell us it was due today!"

"I can't go to gym today, my ankle is killing me."

" You're not going to make us play that stupid game again are you?"

"Man, that's dumb!"

And on and on . . .

Junior Highs which include 7, 8, 9; Middle Schools with 6, 7, 8; schools which are K–5, K–6, K–8 — we've tried them all over the past forty years, yet we're still trying to figure out how best to reach and teach the twelve year old child. Teachers and educators have yet to come up with the perfect environment and program for the beginning of adolescence.

Twelves, caught up in the world of lockers and fifty minute classes are often lost and confused, scared and alone. But in self-contained classrooms, they can appear bored and aloof, disengaged and challenging to adult authority.

The truth may be that there is no perfect place for twelves. For most of my career, I have maintained that twelves (and thirteens and fourteens for that matter) probably do not belong in formal school environments at all, but in something that would be a cross between summer camp and the CCC camps of the Great Depression — plenty of physical activity, structured groups, and time with peers.

Twelves' greatest need is to be with their friends. Teachers and parents take a back seat on the long ride toward the driver's license. The primary developmental struggle is the confusing struggle for identity: the child/not-child begins the search for fidelity in relationships. This is an all-consuming quest beginning at twelve. Minutes turn to hours on the telephone and in front of the mirror. Twelves define themselves by jackets, hairstyles, shoes, CD's, tapes, movies, videos, TV preferences, sports teams, the mall, the dance rage, what older kids are doing. School becomes the place to be, but not always for our intended purposes.

On the other hand, twelves can also become deeply invested

with their peers in purposeful school work. Research projects, current events, environmental issues and causes, scientific experiments, major art projects, dramatic productions can attract and engage the twelve year old.

Sometimes, twelves want fervently to be involved in work as part of a group, and other times want just as fervently to pursue their learning individually. Twelves are changeable, unpredictable and often very hard to read. They often say "That's not what I meant at all!" when an adult misreads a tone of voice, or an off-hand, seemingly rude comment.

Twelve year olds can be offered large doses of responsibility in the school environment and most will respond with pride and accomplishment. Twelves make excellent one-on-one tutors for younger children. They can manage a recycling program for the school, or a school store with help; raise money and goods for needy families; put out a class or school newspaper. They can participate in student councils, organize their first school dance, or plan the spring field trip.

But smaller and more mundane responsibilities, such as keeping their room clean, may elude them. (This, by the way, is *not* the battle to pick with twelves.) At school, keeping track of things like assignments, books, papers, and sweat shirts isn't a priority. Excuses are constant, often transparent and humorous. This ability to be totally responsible and totally irresponsible at the same time can be annoying, even infuriating, to adults. For the twelves, it is simply a matter of priorities. Teachers who hold class meetings and discussions of consequences will be more successful in getting twelves to accept responsibility for their behavior.

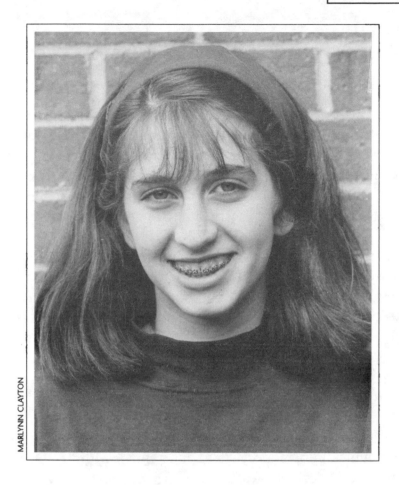

MARLYNN CLAYTON

Physical energy drives twelve year olds. Both boys and girls are now in growth spurts, though puberty comes first to the girls. Both genders, however, require enormous amounts of sleep, food and exercise. Schools don't commonly provide enough time for either of the latter two. Twelves will thrive in a classroom where food is allowed. A mid-morning snack is just as useful to the brain of a twelve year old as that of a five year old and just as essential to their growing bodies. A five minute run around the building or a ten minute game on the playground can rejuvenate and send needed relief to the oxygen-starved brain.

Twelves are excited and challenged by lengthy homework assignments and projects that culminate in visible products: reports with beautiful covers or illustrations; skits about famous people in history, complete with elaborate costumes and props; topographical maps made in three dimensions with chicken wire, papier mâché and paint; scientific models with working parts; computer programs that stump or amaze the class.

Twelves will have reasonable and unreasonable ideas for changing the way the classroom and the school operate. A dress code, chewing gum in school or having a school dance can become major issues. Fairness and the process of making rules become more important. It's important to give twelves an opportunity to discuss and *modify* rules, but it's essential to keep rules consistent and to maintain ultimate adult authority clearly and calmly. Teachers must be fair and firm.

At home, children may seem more introverted and moody, communicate in monosyllables and grunts, withdraw as they sort out their feelings. Teachers can help by providing a view for parents of their children's competence. Sharing children's work with parents is just as important at this age as in kindergarten.

Team sports provide some of the rites of passage twelves need as they enter the teen years. For those not athletically inclined, clubs and activities such as computers, chess, service organizations, Junior Achievement, and scouting can help build bridges into adult-like roles and participation in society. When these rites of passage aren't available, twelves may begin to experiment with the slippery slope of premature sex, violence, alcohol, and drugs, which are clearly portrayed as rites of passage by the media, advertising and many older teens.

Rituals and ceremony can be deeply meaningful to twelve year olds as part of their rites of passage. Confirmation and bat/bar mitzvah have profound meaning and children prepare for these events seriously, with a sense of importance and purpose. Schools can provide similar ceremonial experience through graduations, honor assemblies, service and athletic awards. Twelves and young teens need to see and feel the recognition from adults and their peers that they *are* changing and growing into responsible members of the adult community.

# The Twelve Year Old: Growth Patterns

**Physical**
- High energy
- Much rest needed
- Growth spurt; signs of puberty
- Menstruation for majority of girls
- Food important, especially mid-morning in school
- Physical education and sports valued

**Social**
- Adult personality begins to emerge
- More reasonable, tolerant than at 11
- Enthusiastic, uninhibited
- Will initiate own activity
- Empathetic
- Self-aware, insightful
- Can set realistic goals in the short-term
- Appears secure
- Peers more important than teachers

# The Twelve Year Old: Growth Patterns

**Language**
- Sarcasm emerges
- Double meanings, word play, jokes of intellectual interest
- Enjoys conversation with adults and peers
- Peer "vocabulary" (slang) important

**Cognitive**
- Increased ability to abstract in intellectual pursuits
- May show emerging ability in a particular skill or content area
- Can and will see both sides to an argument
- High interest in current events, politics, social justice; also pop culture, materialism
- Research and study skills advance with increase of organizational discipline

# The Twelve Year Old in the Classroom

**Vision and Fine Motor Ability**

- Increased fine motor ability, patience for practice, self-confidence, makes all fine motor tasks more more pleasurable (see 11 yr. old)
- Sustains reading for long periods; visual concentration better; longer periods on the computer; learns word processing, other skills
- Handwork still popular; interest in more complicated visual-motor tasks (carpentry, mechanical repair, clothes design, architecture)

**Gross Motor Ability**

- Team sports satisfying for many; also individual work in dance, drama, martial arts, gymnastics
- Begin the idea of training, regular exercise, as means to improve physical ability
- Enjoy teaching younger children physical skills

**Cognitive Growth**

- Current events, civics, history highly motivating when tied to issues of clear relevance to students
- More interest and depth in drama, debate, performance; rehearsal and revision increasingly understood, appreciated (true in the writing also)
- Lengthy homework, assignments due over longer periods become more reasonable, but can be problem over weekends; planning and organization of assignments improves

# The Twelve Year Old in the Classroom

**Cognitive Growth**

- Can help peers significantly with subject matter; allow time for peer conferencing, partner projects, lab partners in science, etc.

- Both playful and serious — love to play class games but can have a serious discussion a moment later

- Isolated subject matter, distinct class periods tend to fragment rather than integrate learning; pursue joint teaching projects, self-contained classrooms where possible

**Social Behavior**

- Leadership qualities abound — provide many opportunities for cross-age tutoring, jobs at school, community service, hosting visitors, providing child care for parent meetings

- Teacher should listen, respond to suggestions for changes in routines (as realistic)

- Provide ceremonies, rituals, rewards at significant benchmarks in year; give twelves a part in planning

- Provide access to significant adults (other than teacher) for help with issues of drugs, alcohol, sex, AIDS, violence, family issues

- Making money (from jobs at home, in neighborhood) becomes important

- Make time to listen

# The Twelve Year Old: Curriculum

**Reading**
- Trade books still utilized
- Current events reading through use of newspapers, magazines
- Reading for scientific information; reading of charts, graphs
- Trilogies and book series a favorite
- History, sports, science fiction popular topics
- Interest in fiction with themes tying in to current events/social justice — i.e., *Journey to Johannesburg, Roll of Thunder, Hear My Cry*
- Able to recognize and discuss formal aspects of fiction — setting, character, etc.
- Research reports based on readings from several sources assigned
- Library skills taught: atlas, card catalog, computer searches, etc.

**Writing**
- *Writing* — Revision easier, peer conferences highly effective (certainly useful at all ages); biographies and autobiographic writing; world concern writing: racism, poverty, environmental issues; enjoy a class or school newspaper; writing can be linked to reading program — diaries, fantasies, myths, etc.

# The Twelve Year Old: Curriculum

**Writing**
- *Spelling* — Functional for most; use of "spell checks" for those severely challenged as well as other computer interventions
- *Writing Themes* — Teen issues begin to predominate — sex, drugs and rock and roll, cars; poetry full of emotion; "editorial" writing full of extreme positions; use of "vernacular" or slang in fiction; interesting dialogue; ability to summarize and write briefly with clarity begins to appear
- *Handwriting* — Functional for most; use of word processor taught for all students, even those with good handwriting; letter writing, invitations and thank you notes good practice modes; some students show interest in calligraphy

**Thematic Units** *(Social Studies, Science, Current Events)*
- Politics (including student); current events; community service projects; fund raising (as a theme to be studied); history; racism; elementary economics and statistics; computer simulations; scientific experimentation; the microscopic world

# The Twelve Year Old: Curriculum

**Mathematics**
- Instruction in pre-algebra, extensive use of unknowns
- Using math in science
- Extensive computation in decimals, fractions, percents
- Instruction in geometric problem solving

# Thirteen Year Olds

*"Today I am a teenager. I don't know what I'm feeling right now."*

The Diary of Latoya Hunter: My First Year in Junior High
*by Latoya Hunter*

Life at thirteen can be boring. It can be exciting. It can be frightening. It can be confusing. Most of the time it does seem *quite* confusing to both thirteen year olds as well as parents and teachers.

Thirteen year olds are often "bored," but their outward indifference is driven by what they perceive as the inability of adults to see them as capable young people. "Bored" translates as "insulted." This is not the "scared/bored" of the eight year old, but the challenging "bored" of the adolescent desperately seeking an identity and wanting grown-ups to both notice and leave them alone at the same time. Students at this age who complain that their teachers are "boring" are clearly indicating their perception that they are not being seen, recognized or acknowledged as individuals in the classroom. At the same time, recognition can produce extreme embarrassment — the feeling of being put on the spot.

## Thirteen

Thirteen year olds are excited about the possibilities of the teenage years. Turning thirteen, they express excitement about new freedoms and informal rites of passage — going to the mall *just* with their friends; hanging out; having more control over telephone time; being in an older level school, often with or near the high schoolers; having "harder" subjects such as algebra in school.

Although their excitement at these developments is genuine, thirteens can often be withdrawn — sensitive about their school work as well as their physical appearance. Tentative and hesitant, they desperately need supportive teachers who gently encourage risk-taking in their classrooms.

For females, being thirteen is directly connected to both excitement and apprehension about physical changes, their own developing sexuality and interest shown in them by older adolescent males. By thirteen, the majority of females have begun menstruation and are experiencing all the physical changes of early adolescence. Males, on the other hand, are just beginning to experience signs of puberty at this age. Growth of body hair, genital changes, nocturnal emissions, or other signs of male adolescence emerge as early as eleven in some, but the majority of males will not experience all of these changes until at least 14 or 15 years of age. Nowhere on the developmental continuum is there greater physical and emotional separation between human beings of the same age than between males and females at thirteen.

The confusion that can reign at thirteen reveals itself in dramatic contrasts. There are days of depression where no one likes them, where they do not like themselves. There are days

spent in their rooms — decorating and redecorating, staking out their territory, seeking identity, brooding, being alone. "Leave me alone!" is almost a mantra. Yet, they do not want to be alone for long. There are days of giddiness, of shrieks and shouts. There are days spent in their rooms with friends, with the music turned up, with balls bouncing off walls, of roughhousing and pillow fights.

# Thirteen

THE ROOM at thirteen is the defining space. It provides a clear line of demarcation in the family. It says I am here, but I am moving out. I am here, but I am separate. I am here, but look who I am now! Beginning at thirteen, if not earlier, teenagers' rooms offer interesting developmental indicators as the teenagers design and redesign to reflect their identifications if not their identity.

My own daughter, now in her twenties, remembers her own room's progression: Michael Jackson (8-10); Bon Jovi (11-13); pink walls, a burgundy rug, the Beatles, Marilyn Monroe and "hunk" men on the walls (14-15); white walls, painted collages and written quotes on the walls, pictures of friends, a tapestry on the ceiling (16); black walls, constellations on walls and ceiling (astronomy & physics — not depression — she swears) at 17. Then it was on to college and life in the world of apartments and work.

A meaningful documentation of the icons of adolescence is provided in the powerful photo-essay book *in my room: teenagers in their bedrooms* (Salinger, 1995).

Giving over the bedroom does not mean giving up the child or giving away parental authority, but it does mark a developmental milestone for parents as well as teenagers. It may be the first concrete indicator for parents that things really do need to change on their part as well as their child's. Thus, parents may stop requiring that rooms be "picked-up," but they should also then stop picking up laundry *for* their child. If the room is off limits, then the responsibility for the contents of the room ought also to be off limits, marking increased responsibility along with increased freedom. This, of course, is

PETER WRENN

a key developmental struggle in the creation of a healthy identity: the balance of freedom and responsibility. Parents who are worried about grandparent reactions to messy rooms might initiate an interesting discussion about *their* parents' memories of *their* teenage rooms — and let the current teenager listen in!

Outside their rooms at thirteen, there is also much confusion. In most households the room offers a safe haven, but a parent must also not be afraid to knock and walk in — or ask when a good time to come in might be. Thus the locus of control shifts ever so slightly. Most thirteen year olds desperately want to be able to talk with their parents, but they do not know how to start the conversation. Most parents of thirteen year olds desperately want to talk with their teenagers and, too, often do not know how to begin.

## Thirteen

Learning to listen is among the most important of parenting and teaching skills and is of great value for connecting with those who are thirteen. I have found two books by Adele Faber and Elaine Mazlish of immense help in thinking about how to start and continue meaningful dialogue (Faber and Mazlish, 1980 and 1995).

For most thirteen year olds, school is a series of classrooms, a series of teachers, a rotating series of groups of peers. Contrast this to the stability and insular protection of the room at home. Chris Stevenson, in his excellent book, *Teaching Ten to Fourteen Year Olds* notes about teenagers in school that, "There's no question that they are crying out to be together in settings where they are accepted *and enjoyed by others* (emphasis added). Meanwhile, the organization of large, impersonal schools works against this need by imposing schedules that have students changing classes and classmates every thirty or forty minutes. An eighth grader who felt alienated from her school because the way it was organized kept her separated from many of her friends said cynically, ' I think they're just trying to keep us away from each other so we'll stay confused.'"(Stevenson, 1992, p. 106)

While many middle and junior high schools are now moving to block scheduling and teaming, providing settings where students actually get more social interaction, these schools remain in the minority. The value of social interaction as an intellectual stimulus for teens is not well understood among educators.

It has been documented, across cultures, that cognitive development is greatly enhanced through social interaction.

Cognitive effort is not an isolated or individual activity, despite our emphasis on individual achievement in school. Cognitive growth is enhanced in those environments that foster and respect social interaction — where learners are accepted and enjoyed by others (Rogoff, 1990).

It therefore makes sense that out-of-school activities are especially important to and for thirteen year olds. At thirteen the propensity to hibernate, avoid, stay-by-yourself, stay in your room, and stay on the telephone needs to be countered by opportunities to step out into the new world of school sports, activities, dances, and other structured activities as well as thoughtfully-monitored unstructured peer group time. The majority of thirteen year olds in this country are entering school structures of middle or junior high schools. Sports, activities, student governance and community service offer them the opportunity to engage in cognitive development that helps to build the social and moral strength they will need for the years ahead.

# The Thirteen Year Old: Growth Patterns

**Physical**
- High physical energy
- Skin problems emerging; hygiene a key issue
- Girls: 95% of mature height in average girl; menstruation has begun for most
- Boys: voice change for many; growth spurt about a year behind girls

**Social**
- Neatness a key issue with personal appearance, *not* with personal environment
- The mirror is their best friend and worst enemy
- Often quieter than 12's or 14's
- Like to be alone at home
- Feelings easily hurt and can easily hurt other's feelings
- Mean = scared
- Touchy; flaring anger
- Close friendships more obviously important to girls
- Boys hang in groups or more formal gangs
- Girls more interested in older boys
- Strong sports interest in both genders
- Telephone, computer, video games and other electronic diversions a major time factor

# The Thirteen Year Old: Growth Patterns

**Social**
- Music becoming a major preoccupation
- Peer pressure increasing regarding dress, language, music, in-out, being cool
- Worries about school work
- Humor highlighted by growth of sarcasm
- Horseplay, practical jokes still high in boys
- Collections of things (jewelry, make-up, tapes)

**Language**
- One word answers to adult questions (minimal feedback)
- Street language/peer language important
- Extreme language and volume in face of parental involvement
- Rudeness

**Cognitive**
- Withdrawn and sensitive nature is protective of developing self-concept and intellectual ideas that remain not fully formed
- Abstract reasoning and "formal operations" *begin to be* functional in some 13's
- Tentative approach to difficult intellectual tasks; not willing to take big learning risks
- Like to challenge intellectual as well as social authority

# The Thirteen Year Old in the Classroom

**Motor Skills**
- Boys awkward, girls more agile
- Upper body strength lacking in both boys and girls
- Too much close eye work may cause headaches and fatigue

**Cognitive**
- Interest in man's inhumanity to man; issues of fairness and justice; have a desire to serve others
- Interest in particular subjects begins to differentiate as most change classes for each subject
- Afraid of journal writing, revealing too much
- Can enjoy reading and writing of subject matter, tend to hate grammar and spelling
- Often write better than they speak — inwardized age does not respond well in class discussions — oral presentation — exception to this would be in the area of drama
- Short, regular, predictable homework assignments build study habits, successful routines
- Self-evaluation of work helpful to balance teacher evaluation and grading of work at this self-critical age
- Begin to enjoy thinking about the many sides to an issue or solution to a problem

# The Thirteen Year Old in the Classroom

**Social**

- Will not do as well in cooperative groups as 12's or older teens — tend to argue, complain about fairness
- Enjoy solitary activity in the classroom or working with a single partner on a project
- Want to know " Why do we have to learn this?"
- Bus behavior can be very problematic or out-of-control, especially for boys
- Gym (including dressing and showering), health, sex ed classes often embarrassing and lead to silly or acting out or rude behavior in class
- Highly critical of teachers (judgmental) either positively or negatively. . . pass on reputations
- Think globally, but still can't often act locally; i.e., often mean to each other

# The Thirteen Year Old: Curriculum

**Reading**
- Fiction and nonfiction reading involving social issues work well
- Extensive study of literary elements — plot, character, mood, setting, and theme
- Class read-alouds, especially around social topics (conformity, personal safety, homelessness) are a useful springboard to discussion and better understanding
- Concentration on acquisition of vocabulary — from context as well as dictionary and thesaurus use
- Documentation of statements based on textual reference is encouraged

**Writing**
- *Writing* — Ability to handle revision with careful attention paid to the difference between critique and personal criticism; pride in "proper" form and mechanics of writing; can begin to structure short (one page) expository essays with attention to thesis statement and supporting details; ability to summarize can be honed with précis writing

# The Thirteen Year Old: Curriculum

**Writing**
- *Spelling* — Functional for most; spell checkers and word processing programs for those still experiencing difficulty are an essential tool
- *Writing Themes* — Much writing springs from study of themes and topics arising in curricular literature readings; stories often revolve around social "peer" issues and involve issues of justice and injustice, inclusion and exclusion
- *Handwriting* — Functional for most; word processors essential for those still having difficulty and extremely valuable for all students, particularly as they ease the task of revision

**Thematic Units**
*(Social Studies, Science, Current Events)*
- Issues of resource use which are visible in students' lives (waste generation, disposal, recycling; energy generation and use; hunger, and the growth, distribution, and consumption of food); Historical conflicts with reflection on their resolution and impact (slavery, the clash of Native American and European cultures, American Revolution); Historical biographies; Study of the composition of building materials of our physical world (water, air, soil)

# The Thirteen Year Old: Curriculum

**Mathematics** • Review all operations with special emphasis on conversion of decimals, fractions, percents

- Mathematical set-making and attribute mapping — study of number patterns and sequences (i.e., Fibonacci, Binary, Geometric, etc.)

- Extensive and sophisticated use of geometric tools (compass and straight edge) to construct and organize space

- Development of a 30-word geometric vocabulary

- Mathematical conversations about the concept of zero and negative numbers

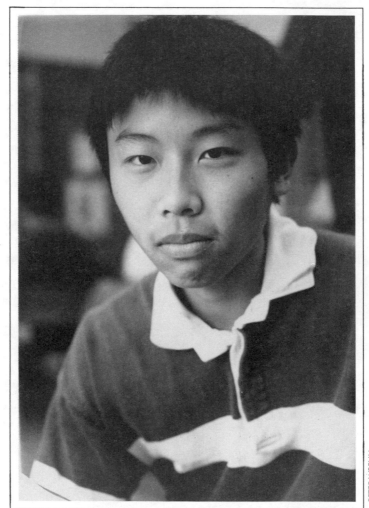

# Fourteen Year Olds

*"I'm kind of small for fourteen
even though I have a good build,
and those guys were bigger than me."*

The Outsiders
*by S.E. Hinton*

Now it's time for the boys to spend hours in front of the mirror. Aware of their physical changes and increasingly aware of the girls around them, many fourteen year old boys are entering puberty. Most of the girls are already there.

Fourteen year olds of both genders put enormous physical, emotional and cognitive energy into the development of an adolescent subculture. "Distancing" from the grown-ups is the name of their dance. Just as their bedrooms mirror the image teens are trying on, so too their clothes, hairstyle, music and language create a "portable mirror" for them as they move around in school, on the street or at the mall. The mirror attracts other teens, but tends to put off adults.

## Fourteen

Erik Erikson, whose theory remains our primary source of understanding for social and emotional growth, noted in 1968 that adolescents often seem, "preoccupied with what they appear to be in the eyes of others as compared with what they feel they are . . ." (Erikson, 1968, p. 128). Adolescence is the time in which the developing person is beginning to focus on the issue of personal *identity* — the "who am I?" question that we all ask. At fourteen, "who I am" seems to be defined by "who we are." The portable mirror of the peer group is a more easily understood reflection of self.

Fourteen year olds are beginning to move away from parents and teachers as the central figures in their lives. When I asked thirteen and fourteen year olds about what people they would seek advice from about a serious problem, both ages mentioned their parents, but it was the fourteen year olds who also said they would consult their best friends. This distancing from parents is also seen in the awkward embarrassment at this age of being seen with parents, of parents dressing "poorly," of having an old car, of parents saying the wrong thing.

Challenging the authority of the adult now becomes almost a visceral reaction. Note the increase of challenges and opposition toward teachers at this age. Students often take the opposite side of an intellectual idea or opinion from that of the adult, and seem many times to argue for arguing's sake. Fourteen year olds want to do it their way, to have freedom, to be on their own. This typically-teen behavior often peaks at fifteen.

At fourteen, adolescents are looking constantly for opportunities to decide by themselves what they will do on their own — such as obtain a part-time job, play a sport, join a rock band — "and at the same time are mortally afraid of being forced into activities in which they would feel exposed to ridicule or self-doubt" (Erikson, 1968, p. 129). Such activities might include going out to eat with parents or dressing up.

Developmental psychologist Jeanette Haviland-Jones points out that what often appears as adolescent embarrassment (such as eye-rolling, teeth sucking, hair tossing and the like) in reaction to parents or teachers, is actually adolescent mimicking of adult behavior — more of the "distancing dance" of the teenager. Haviland-Jones calls this way of acting "contempt" and defines it as the social skill which in adult company keeps us safely and appropriately apart from one another, which helps us to establish our own psychological space (*Responsive Leadership Forum* presentation, Greenfield, MA, July 1996).

This behavior is part of what adolescents use to establish their emerging adult identity and to work on what Erikson calls the struggle of each adolescent: the search for *fidelity*. By fidelity he means "disciplined devotion" to an emerging sense of self, to some other person or persons, to ideas or fads. Fourteen year olds can exhibit this intense devotion to a sport in which they engage or to a drug, to a musical instrument or to body piercing (sometimes to both), to a friendship or to a gang, to an idol or to idleness. All of this practice around issues of fidelity is in anticipation of grown-up participation as a devoted, disciplined, loving and caring reproductive partner and as a full-fledged citizen of a homeland.

The successful development of the virtue of fidelity is dependent not only on the individual teen, but also on the guidelines, customs, cultural mores, and rites of passage provided by family, heritage and the society at large. When we think about rites of passage for fourteen year olds, few come to mind. Confirmation and bar/bat mitzvahs usually come at a slightly younger age for those who have them. The driver's license is still years away. Some schools provide "Project Adventure" type experiences which provide passages such as solo hikes, high ropes courses, and other high challenge in a safe, structured environment. Summer camps which provide similar experiences or move fourteen year olds into Counselor-in-Training positions also structure "passage" experiences. Some parents are now developing and creating family "passage parties" where the childhood of the adolescent is reviewed and celebrated and the dawning adulthood is honored and acknowledged. All such passage experiences help the adolescent think about and practice what it means to be devoted to oneself and to others in a disciplined way.

Though family, church, camps, and other social arenas are important, society for the fourteen year old is primarily school. School is the structured social setting where the external society makes its demands on the adolescent. How the school is structured and how it places demands on its students is of critical importance in the development of healthy young adults for our future society.

Take the demand of homework. Many fourteen year olds will tell you they wish they didn't have homework, that their lives are busy enough after school as it is with work, taking care of younger siblings, or sports and activities that keep them out late. Homework seems like busy-work. They resent it and don't see the point of it, except that it lowers their grades if they don't get it done and might mean detention and the inability to participate in after-school activities. How they respond to this educational ritual and demand is dependent on the way teachers and parents structure the demand and respond to challenges about it. If adults understand the need of the fourteen year old to challenge this structure, and respond with understanding and a spirit of negotiation, then the fourteen year old will be able to demonstrate "disciplined devotion" to homework and to those adults who treat them in this respectful way. If, however, homework is meted out as menial work or punishment, fourteen year olds will resist and rebel in ways that will not lead to disciplined devotion about homework or to the generalization of devotion to other ultimately productive tasks.

One positive way to deal with homework for a rebellious teen is for the teacher to engage in active bargaining about the amount of homework they think the student can accomplish on a given night in the teacher's subject area. Thus, the student will not be assigned the same amount of homework as other students each night, but will be challenging himself to do his personal best. A student who bargains for three math problems one night will be given three problems, with the teacher helping her to understand that the next night the minimum will be four and so on. This "incremental success" approach to homework is respectful of individual differences and needs, yet also respectful of high standards by increasing accountability inch by inch. Teachers should also have such students keep a visual record or graph of their homework ups and downs. This approach can also be effective with those highly motivated and conscientious students who always ask for thirty problems every night. A teacher might help such students realize that once in a while they might have a night where they have too many outside obligations and that it is all right sometimes not to kill themselves by staying up till two in the morning to get thirty problems done. This would be a meaningful lesson, not to mention a surprise for such responsible students. This is one example of how adults can help to make adolescent issues a building ground instead of a battle ground.

PETER WRENN

This scenario can also be repeated in regard to the adolescent's response to in-school assignments, participation in sports, chores at home, thank you notes to grandparents, curfews. Each encounter offers the adolescent apprenticeship in adulthood through respectful interaction with caring adults.

How can we create more positive demands, rites of passages and rituals in our schools and at home? In both places, the more we create structures that allow us to take the time to truly listen to the ideas of fourteen year olds, the more chance there is that fidelity will emerge. Listening to our fourteen year olds is not the same thing as giving in to their demands. Listening means confirming their experience, acknowledging their presence, helping them to be in settings where they are accepted and enjoyed by teachers and parents.

At school this means setting aside more time in middle school for "advisories," counseling, peer tutoring, community service and academic performance assessment. These have to stop being seen as add-on's to an old-fashioned, outmoded rigid system of subject matter accountability and start being seen as the proper structures in school for healthy and productive adolescent growth and development. Our traditional model of schooling for young adolescents is built on the assumption that a miniature high school or college environment will teach the students what they need to get ready for as adults. What it misses is the critical understanding that adolescents cannot get ready for the future by living in it.

Adolescents must *work through and internalize the capacity for fidelity* in order to be able some day to participate as competent adults. Until we heed this admonition we will continue to reap the chaos of confusion that is the legacy of most of today's middle schools. It is the structures we create, not the struggles of youth that are responsible for the future. Adults must take the responsibility and make the necessary investments to look at time, teaching and relationship with adolescents through new eyes.

At home, this investment of time is equally critical. Despite the fact that fourteen year olds want to spend *all* their time on the phone, at the mall, or with their friends, we must not give away our adult responsibility to set aside family time on a regular, structured schedule for listening and discussion. We also must not be intimidated by the threats and tears of our teenagers when we do so. It is hard, but we must be the adults. "Family Meetings" are one popular format for allowing discussion and decision-making by all members of the family (Nelsen, 1996). More informal listening time — the knock on the door of the sacred bedroom — is also important. And try to resist the temptation to talk with your teenager when anger is in the air. This is not the time to exert your adult power; instead exercise your adult restraint and set up a time to talk later when you are both cooled down. As adults, we are the ones who should be capable of showing disciplined devotion to our teenagers as they are working through and learning this virtue. By our example, we provide guidance even as our children seem to push us away.

Often as fourteen turns into fifteen, a seemingly greater gulf begins to be felt between parent and teenager, teacher and adolescent student. The following letter is a real-life example:

*Dear Mom and Dad,*

*The reason I'm writing this letter is simply because spoken words do **NOT** seem to get through; I try to talk to you and sometimes you listen but other times . . .*

*You say that you're the adult and that you're in control but part of being in control is being able to listen to other people and be willing to make some changes.*

*I'm not a little girl and to be honest I don't even consider myself a "child" anymore. Maybe by my* birthdate I'm not old enough to make important decisions about **MY** life. But looking at my maturity and intelligence levels, I think it's about time you let me be in control of my life.

It seems like you guys have this thing with power. Like having power and control over my life is your ultimate goal.

If you don't let me go now, when you finally do, I won't come back. You're showering me with too many limits and too much of your protective "love." You're both driving me away.

If this is how it's going to be how it is until I turn 21 or even 16 I don't want to be a part of it or a part of your lives. I love you mom and dad, but I'm sick of the way I'm being treated. Don't my feelings count too?!

I've been thinking a lot about "running away." And if that's the only way I can get through to you, I will do it!! There are plenty of places that I can go. This is not a threat so you will say, "okay, do whatever you want." These are the facts, the way things are going to be until you let me go to live my own life. It's your choice.

**MY** life and well-being are as important to me as they are to you. Let **ME** be in control. It's **MY** life.

> "Some men see things as they are and say why, I
> dream things that never were and say why not"
> W.J.

— your daughter

Sometimes it is hard to have the appropriate listening skills. But we need to understand that emotions such as those expressed by this fifteen year old are both a pushing away and a deep desire to remain connected, all a part of the struggle for fidelity. Fidelity — to parents and teachers — can certainly re-emerge as one of the blessings of our relationships with our older adolescents.

# The Fourteen Year Old: Growth Patterns

**Physical**
- High energy continues
- Generally healthy age — pushes through illness in desire to participate with peers
- Loud
- Alcohol and drugs a major influence on physical well being
- Girls; full development nearly complete
- Boys; growth spurt continues
- Both; sexually active in increasing percentages
- Upper body strength begins to develop in boys
- High need for physical exercise and snacking

**Social**
- Like to do as much as possible — cram as much into the day as they can
- More of their own adult personality evident
- Often embarrassed to be seen with their parents; critical of parental dress, habits, friends, ideas
- Loud
- Especially don't like or respond well to adult lectures; feel that they know what is going to be said once a few words have been spoken; "know it all" stage
- Can be a pain at home and a star at school

# The Fourteen Year Old: Growth Patterns

**Language**
- Peer language patterns of paramount importance, but learning to negotiate adult world as well
- Will engage more in group discussion
- Interested in the meaning of words; developing a broader vocabulary
- Loud

**Cognitive**
- More abstract reasoning evident, especially in regard to cause and effect
- More willing to admit an error, revise their work or try something a second or a third time
- Very aware of problems in larger world and generally still invested in finding solutions and participating in learning more
- Interested in technology and how things work
- Learn well in cooperative groups
- Respond well to academic variety and challenge
- Easily "bored"

# The Fourteen Year Old in the Classroom

**Motor Skills** • Need as much physical release as possible; brief periods out of doors, run around the playground; stretch break in the classroom

• Posture and ability to sit "properly" in typical school furniture is difficult; do well when allowed to lounge or sprawl on floor for certain amount of class time

• A rest period, quiet reading, nap, often improves performance and behavior in the afternoon

• Normally loud. . . balance in classroom expectations is important; silence sometimes, but not all the time

**Cognitive** • Function well in small (8-10) person discussion groups or cooperative learning groups (smaller)

• Like to improve work if given the chance to revise efforts - can be self-critical and also help effectively in peer conferencing in any subject area

• Interested in study of psychology. . . "Who am I?"

• Enjoy and do well with lengthier project assignments

# The Fourteen Year Old in the Classroom

**Cognitive**
- Enjoy research and putting together research reports including format
- Increased interest in math and science for many
- Current events a popular subject and often discussed either formally or informally
- Interest in manual skills, musical skills, artistic skills, and other ways of expressing particular intelligence emerging in the adult mind

**Social**
- Complain about *volume* of homework, but often secretly enjoy challenge and their ability to meet teacher demands
- Often say work is too easy when they find it *plenty* challenging
- Complain about work as "boring" — translate as: "I don't really understand this stuff."
- In some school settings give in to peer pressure not to do well in school, be a "nerd"
- Service projects, student government, class dances, sporting events and other group undertakings are of major significance often leading to a first career interest
- Humor more differentiated; can be extremely funny, creative

# The Fourteen Year Old: Curriculum

**Reading**

- Many genres are represented — song lyrics, poetry, drama, short story, as well as novels

- Themes of literature serve as a wonderful vehicle for development of perspective on self and others as quest for identity intensifies

- Begin to understand the interweaving of literary elements — how characterization can forward the plot of a story, for example

- Difference between fact and opinion is explored as textual references are emphasized in writing and discussion

- Understanding the use of language as tool for different purposes (for example a study of advertising language)

- Class read-alouds continue to appeal and serve as springboard for discussion

- Vocabulary study continues and becomes more sophisticated; some are ready to enjoy the logic of analogies

# The Fourteen Year Old: Curriculum

**Writing**
- *Writing* — Students choose appropriate genre (poem, play, story) in which to represent their ideas; students also "try out" different voices, often tied in with literature being studied; writing from different points of view is a useful exercise; students more deliberately use grammatical constructions for stylistic reasons; use of conventional footnotes, endnotes, and bibliographic entries introduced

- *Spelling* — Functional for most; those still having difficulty must use spell checkers and word processors as a tool

- *Writing Themes* — Writing to prepare for debates and "mock trial" sorts of activities are a great motivator as students continue to develop the ability to structure and defend their thinking; the universal themes of literature provide a springboard for writing assignments and for creative writing; journals with adults are important places for students to reflect as they struggle to define themselves and to sort out issues in their own lives and in the larger world; longer research papers related to thematic studies are appropriate

- *Handwriting* — Fluency with word processor becomes even more critical

# The Fourteen Year Old: Curriculum

**Thematic Units**
*(Social Studies, Science, Current Events)*

- Physical and human geography; current world conflicts with emphasis upon causality and resolution; the intersection of natural resource use and current lifestyles (water — its structure, characteristics and use; weather and the impact of the greenhouse effect; oil, the rainforest, and indigenous lifestyles); basic physical and biological principles (power of the crowbar, dynamics of flight, osmosis and transport of water in trees)

**Mathematics**

- Review all operations with special emphasis on ratio and proportion
- Reading and utilizing graphs, particularly circle and bar graphs
- Exploration of different bases — binary number system
- Solving equations with a single unknown
- Study of functions — interaction of two variables
- Instruction in formal algebra begins for many

# References

Ashton-Warner, S. (1971). *Teacher*. New York, NY: Bantam.

Charney, R., Clayton, M. K., Finer, M., Lord, J., Wood, R. (1993). *A Notebook for Teachers: Making Changes in the Elementary Curriculum*. Greenfield, MA: Northeast Foundation for Children, Inc.

Cleary, B. (1968). *Ramona The Pest*. New York, NY: Avon Books.

Cohen, M. (1980). *First Grade Takes a Test*. New York, NY: William Morrow & Co., Inc.

Comer, J. P., Poussaint, A. F. (1992). *Raising Black Children*. New York, NY: Penguin Books.

Erikson, E. H. (1968). *Identity: Youth and Crisis*. New York, NY: W.W. Norton & Company, Inc.

Faber, A., Mazlish, E. (1995). *How to Talk So Kids Can Learn: At Home and in School*. New York, NY: Simon & Schuster.

Faber, A., Mazlish, E. (1980). *How to Talk So Kids Will Listen & Listen So Kids Will Talk*. New York, NY: Avon Books.

Gilligan, C. (1982). *In a Different Voice*. Cambridge, MA: Harvard University Press.

Hale-Benson, J. E. (1982). *Black Children: Their Roots, Culture, and Learning Styles*. Baltimore, MD: The Johns Hopkins University Press.

Konner, M. (1991). *Childhood: A Multicultural View*. Boston, MA: Little, Brown and Co.

McAdoo, H. P., McAdoo, J. L. (1985). *Black Children: Social, Educational, and Parental Environments*. Beverly Hills, CA: Sage Publications.

Mitchell, L. S. (1934). *Young Geographers*. New York, NY: Bank Street College of Education.

Nelsen, J. (1996). *Positive Discipline*. New York, NY: Ballantine Books.

Rogoff, B. (1990). *Apprenticeship in Thinking: Cognitive Development in Social Context*. New York, NY: Oxford University Press.

Salinger, A. (1995). *in my room: teenagers in their bedrooms*. San Francisco, CA: Chronicle Books.

Stevenson, C. (1992). *Teaching Ten to Fourteen Year Olds*. White Plains, NY: Longman Publishing Group.

# Some Favorite Books for Different Ages

Favorite titles from the author, and teachers and children at the Greenfield Center School.

## Books for Fours, Fives and Sixes

*Abiyoyo*, by Pete Seeger, New York: Scholastic Inc., 1963.

*And the Relatives Came*, by Cynthia Rylant, New York: Macmillan, 1985.

*A is for Africa*, by Ife Nii Owoo, Africa World Young Readers, 1992.

*Blueberries for Sal*, by Robert McCloskey, New York: Scholastic Inc., 1948.

*Bringing the Rain to Kapiti Plain*, by Verna Aardema, New York: Penguin, 1981.

*The Carrot Seed*, by Ruth Krauss, New York: Harper & Row, 1945.

*The Caterpillar and the Polliwog*, by Jack Kent, New York: Random Books for Young Readers, 1985.

*Cloudy With a Chance of Meatballs*, by Judi Barrett, New York: Atheneum, 1978.

*First Grade Takes a Test*, by Miriam Cohen, New York: William Morrow & Co., Inc., 1980.

*Frederick*, by Leo Lionni, New York: Pantheon Books (Random House), 1967.

*Go Dog Go,* by P. D. Eastman, New York: Random House, 1961.

*Henry and Mudge*, by Cynthia Rylant, New York: Macmillan, 1987.

*Ibis, A True Whale Story*, by John Himmelman, New York: Scholastic, Inc., 1990.

*If You Give A Mouse A Cookie*, by Laura Numeroff, New York: Scholastic, Inc., 1985.

*It's About Cats*, by Gallimard Jeunesse, New York: Scholastic, Inc., 1989.

*A Kiss For Little Bear*, by Else H. Minarik, New York: Harper Collins Children's Books, 1984.

*The Little Mouse, The Red Ripe Strawberry, and the Hungry Bear*, by Don and Audrey Wood, Singapore: Child's Play International, 1984.

*The Lorax*, by Dr. Seuss, New York: Random House, 1961.

*Lost*, by Jay Cowley, San Diego: Shortland Publications, 1981.

*No Fighting, No Biting*, by Else H. Minarik, New York: Harper Collins Children's Books, 1978.

*Owl Moon*, Jane Yolen, New York: Putnam Publishing, 1987.

*The Party*, by Jay Cowley, San Diego: Shortland Publications, 1983.

*Pearl's Pirates*, by Frank Asch, New York: Dell, 1989.

*The Rainbow Fish*, by Marcus Pfister, New York: North-South Books, 1992.

*Rainbow Goblins*, by Ulde Rico, New York: Warner, 1978.

*Roxaboxen*, by Alice Mclerran, Wooster, OH: Lathrop, 1991.

*Sheep in a Jeep*, by Nancy Shaw, New York: Houghton, 1986.

*The Sneetches*, by Dr. Seuss, New York: Random House, 1971.

*A Trio for Grandpapa*, by Shulamith Oppenheim, New York: Thomas Crowell, 1974.

*Two by Two*, by Barbara Reid, New York: Scholastic, Inc., 1992.

*The Vanishing Pumpkin*, by Tony Johnston, New York: Scholastic, Inc., 1983.

*The Very Hungry Caterpillar*, by Eric Carle, New York: Putnam Publishing Group, 1981.

# Books for Sevens and Eights

*All About Sam*, by Lois Lowry, Boston: Houghton Mifflin, 1988.

*The BFG*, by Roald Dahl, London: Penguin Group, 1982.

*The Boxcar Children Series*, by Gertrude Chandler Warner, New York: Scholastic, Inc., 1989.

*Catwings*, by Ursula K. LeGuin, New York: Orchard Books, 1988.

*CDB!*, by William Steig, New York: S & S Trade, 1987.

*Charlie and the Chocolate Factory*, by Roald Dahl, New York: Alfred A. Knopf, 1964.

*Charlotte's Web*, by E.B. White, New York: Harper & Row, 1953.

*Dominic*, by William Steig, New York: Collins, 1972.

*Fantastic Mr. Fox*, by Roald Dahl, New York: Puffin, 1988.

*George Washington's Socks*, by Elvira Woodruff, New York: Scholastic, Inc., 1991.

*The Haunted House*, by Dorothy Haas, New York: Scholastic, Inc., 1988.

*The Haunting of Grade Three*, by Grace Maccarone, New York: Scholastic, Inc., 1984.

*James and the Giant Peach*, by Roald Dahl, New York: Knopf Books for Young Readers, 1961.

*Karen's Witch*, by Ann M. Martin, New York: Scholastic Apple Paperbacks, 1988.

*Little House in the Big Woods*, by Laura Ingalls Wilder, New York: Harper & Row, 1945.

*The Little Mermaid*, by Deborah Hautzig, New York: Random House, 1991.

*The Littles and the Terrible Tiny Kid*, by John Peterson, New York: Scholastic, Inc., 1993.

*Matilda*, by Roald Dahl, New York: The Penguin Group, 1988.

*Midnight Express*, by Margaret Wetteren, Minneapolis: Carolrhoda Books, 1990.

*Mystery in the Night Woods*, by John Peterson, New York: Scholastic, Inc., 1991.

*Nate the Great Series* by Marjorie Sharmat, New York: Dell, 1972.

*The Rag Coat*, by Lauren Mills, Boston: Little Brown and Co., 1991.

*Ramona The Pest, Ramona Quimby: Age 8* and other *Ramona* books by Beverly Cleary, New York: Avon Books, 1968.

*Scary Stories*, by Alvin Schwartz, New York: Harper Collins, 1981.

*The Story of Babe Ruth; Baseball's Greatest Legend*, by Lisa Eisenberg, New York: Dell Yearling Biography, 1990.

*Stuart Little*, by E.B. White, New York: Harper & Row, 1945.

*The Tree of Freedom*, by Rebeca Caudill, New York: Scholastic, 1947.

*23 Multicultural Tales to Tell*, by Pleasant de Spain, Arkansas: August House, 1993.

*The Witch and the Ring* by Ruth Chew, New York: Peter Smith, 1992.

*Yuck Soup Story*, by Joy Cowley, Bothell, WA: Wright Group, 1986.

*Zlateh the Goat and Other Stories*, by Isaac Singer, New York: Harper Trophy, 1984.

## Books for Nines and Tens

*Anastasia Has The Answers*, by Lois Lowry, New York: Dell, 1987.

*Anastasia Krupnik*, by Lois Lowry, New York: Bantam, 1979.

*The Brightest Light*, by Colleen O. McKenna, New York: Scholastic, Inc., 1992.

*The Chalk Doll*, by Charlotte Pomerantz, New York: Harper-Collins, 1993.

*Chronicles of Narnia*, by C.S. Lewis, New York: Scholastic, Inc., 1953.

*Double Play*, by Matt Christopher, Canada: Little, Brown & Co., 1964 (and any other Matt Christopher sports books).

*Emily's Runaway Imagination*, by Beverly Cleary, New York: Avon Books, 1985.

*The Fourth Grade Wizards* and *Nothing's Fair in Fifth Grade*, by Barthe DeClements, New York: Puffin Books, 1988 & 1990.

*From the Mixed-Up Files of Mrs. Basil E. Frankenweiler*, by E.L. Konigsburg, New York: Macmillan, 1987.

*The Great Brain at the Academy*, by John D. Fitzgerald, New York: Dell, 1972.

*Hare's Choice*, by Dennis Hamley, New York: Dell Yearling, 1988.

*The Indian in the Cupboard Series*, by Lynn Reid Banks, New York: Doubleday, Inc., 1987.

*Jeremy Thatcher, Dragon Hatcher*, by Bruce Coville, New York: Pocket Books, 1991.

*King of the Wind*, by Marguerite Henry, Chicago: McNally and Company, 1948.

*Little House on the Prairie*, by Laura Ingalls Wilder, New York: Scholastic, Inc., 1935.

*Mrs. Frisby and the Rats of NIMH*, by Robert C. O'Brien, New York: Macmillan Publishing Co., 1971.

*My Father's Dragon* and *Elmer the Dragon* and *The Dragons of Blueland*, by Ruth Stiles Gannett, New York: Knopf, 1986, 1987, 1963.

*My Teacher is an Alien*, by Bruce Coville, New York: Minstrel Books, 1989.

*Otis Spofford*, by Beverly Cleary, New York: Avon Books, 1953.

*Peter and the Wolf*, by Sergei Prokofiev, New York: Knopf, 1986.

*Pippi Goes On Board*, by Astrid Lindgren, New York: Puffin Books, 1977.

*Ralph S. Mouse*, by Beverly Cleary, New York: Dell, 1982.

*The Revenge of the Wizard's Ghost*, by John Bellairs, New York: Bantam Skylark, 1986.

*Song of the Trees*, by Mildred D. Taylor, New York: Bantam, 1971.

*Tales of a Fourth Grade Nothing*, by Judy Blume, New York: Dell Yearling, 1972.

*Volcano*, by Meryl Siegman, New York: Bantam, 1987.

*Walk When The Moon Is Full*, by Frances Hamerstrom, Freedom, CA: The Crossing Press, 1975.

## Books for Elevens and Twelves

*A Connecticut Yankee in King Arthur's Court*, by Mark Twain, New York: Bantam, 1983.

*The Adventures of Tom Sawyer*, by Mark Twain, New York: Bantam, 1983.

*Black Beauty*, by Anna Sewell, Toronto: Random House, 1990.

*Blood Root*, by Doug Hobbie, New York: Crown Publishers, 1991.

*The Book of Three*, by Lloyd Alexander, New York: Holt, Rinehart & Winston, 1964.

*The Borning Room*, by Paul Fleishman, New York: Scholastic, 1991.

*Bridge to Terabithia*, by Katherine Paterson, New York: Harper Collins, 1977.

*Charlie and the Chocolate Factory*, by Roald Dahl, New York: Penguin Books, 1964.

*Children of the Wolf*, by Jane Yolen, New York: The Penguin Group, 1984.

*Comet in Moominland*, by Tove Jansson, Canada: Harper Collins Canada Ltd., 1991.

*The Devil's Arithmetic*, by Jane Yolen, New York: Puffin Books, 1988.

*Dragons of the Lost Sea*, by Laurence Yep, New York: Harper Trophy, 1982.

*Dragon Singer*, by Anne McCaffrey, New York: Bantam, 1978.

*The Egypt Game*, by Zilpha Snyder, New York: Atheneum Childrens Books, 1967.

*The Friendship; The Gold Cadillac*, by Mildred Taylor, New York: Bantam Skylark Books, 1989.

*The Girl on the Outside*, by Mildred Pitts Walker, New York: Scholastic, 1993.

*Ghosts I Have Been*, by Richard Peck, New York: Dell, 1992.

*Harriet the Spy*, by Louise Fitzhugh, New York: Harper Collins Publishers, 1964.

*The Hobbitt*, by J.R.R. Tolkien, New York: Houghton Mifflin, 1984.

*A Horse Called Holiday*, by Frances Wilbur, New York: Scholastic, Inc., 1992.

*The Little Prince*, by Antoine de Saint-Exupery, New York: Harcourt Brace Jovanovich, Inc., 1971.

*Number the Stars*, by Lois Lowry, New York: Dell Publishing, 1990.

*Redwall Series*, by Brian Jacques, New York: Avon, 1991.

*The Riddle Master Of Hed*, by Patricia A. McKillip, New York: Ballantine Books, 1978.

*The Search for Delicious*, by Natalie Babbitt, Canada: Harper Collins Ltd., 1969.

*A Sending of Dragons*, by Jane Yolen, New York: Dell Publishing, 1987.

*Sixth Grade Secrets*, by Louis Sachar, New York: Scholastic, Inc., 1987.

*Snow Treasure*, by Marie McSwigan, New York: Scholastic, Inc., 1942.

*A Swiftly Tilting Planet*, by Madeleine L'Engle, New York: Dell Publishing, 1978.

*The Truth About Sixth Grade*, by Colleen O. McKenna, New York: Scholastic, Inc., 1991.

*The Upstairs Room and the Journey Home*, by Johanna Reiss, New York: Harper Row Publishers, 1990.

*The Vampire's Promise*, by Caroline B. Cooney, New York: Scholastic, Inc., 1993.

*Witches*, by Roald Dahl, New York: Puffin Books, 1988.

*The Wizard in the Hall*, by Lloyd Alexander, New York: Dell, 1975.

*A Wrinkle in Time*, by Madeleine L'Engle, New York: Dell, 1962.

## Books for Thirteens and Fourteens

*Allegra Maud Goldman*, by Edith Konecky, New York: Dell, 1976.

*Annie John*, by Jamaica Kincaid, NAL-Dutton, 1986.

*Anpao*, by Jamake Highwater, New York: Harper-Collins, 1992.

*Arm of the Starfish*, by Madeleine L'Engle, New York: Bantam-Doubleday-Dell, 1980.

*The Chocolate War*, by Robert Cormier, New York: Bantam-Doubleday-Dell, 1974.

*David and Jonathan*, by Cynthia Voight, New York: Scholastic, 1992.

*A Day No Pigs Would Die*, by Robert Newton Peck, New York: Dell, 1972.

*The Diary of Adrian Mole*, by Sue Townsend, New York: Avon, 1982.

*The Diary of Latoya Hunter*, by Latoya Hunter, New York: Vintage Books, 1992.

*Fallen Angels*, by Walter Dean Myers, New York: Scholastic, 1989.

*The Farthest Shore*, by Ursula LeGuin, New York: Bantam-Doubleday-Dell, 1984.

*The Giver*, by Lois Lowry, New York: Bantam-Doubleday-Dell, 1994.

*Good-Bye and Keep Cold*, by Jenny Davis, Orchard Books, 1987.

*House of Dies Drear*, by Virginia Hamilton, New York: Aladdin, 1968.

*The House on Mango Street*, by Sandra Cisneros, New York: Random, 1991.

*I Heard the Owl Call My Name*, by Margaret Craven, New York: Dell, 1980.

*Make Lemonade*, by Virginia Euwer Wolff, New York: Scholastic, 1994.

*Meet the Austins*, by Madeleine L'Engle, New York: Bantam-Doubleday-Dell, 1981.

*The Monument*, by Gary Paulsen, New York: Dell, 1991.

*Never Cry Wolf*, by Farley Mowat, New York: Bantam-Doubleday-Dell, 1983.

*Nothing But the Truth*, by Avi, New York: Avon, 1993.

*The Outsiders*, by S.E. Hinton, New York: Dell Publishing, 1967.

*Roll of Thunder, Hear My Cry*, by Mildred Taylor, New York: Bantam, 1978.

*The Runner*, by Cynthia Voight, New York: Scholastic, 1985.

*Scorpions*, by Walter Dean Myers, New York: Harper-Collins, 1988.

*A Stranger in the Kingdom*, by Howard Mosher, New York: Dell, 1990.

*Watership Down*, by Richard Adams, New York: Avon, 1972.

# Books for Parents and Teachers

## General Resources

*Adolescence: The Survival Guide for Parents and Teenagers.* Elizabeth Fenwick and Dr. Tony Smith. New York: DK Publishing, Inc., 1996. (A) (P)

*Ages and Stages: Developmental Descriptions & Activities, Birth Through Eight Years.* Karen Miller. Chelsea, MA: Teleshare Publishing Company, 1985. (C) (P)

*Apprenticeship in Thinking: Cognitive Development in Social Context.* Barbara Rogoff. New York: Oxford University Press, 1990. (C) (A)

---

*A letter designation has been added after each book to indicate:*
*(C) Books about children's development*
*(A) Books about adolescent development*
*(P) Books of interest to parents*
*All books are appropriate for teachers*

---

*Arnold Gesell: Themes of His Work*. Louise Bates Ames, Ph.D. New York: Human Sciences Press, 1989. (A)

*A to Z Guide to Your Child's Behavior: A Parent's Easy and Authoritative Reference to Hundreds of Everyday Problems and Concerns From Birth to 12 Years*. Compiled by the faculty of the Children's National Medical Center, under the direction of David Mrazek, M.D. and William Garrison, Ph.D., with Laura Elliott. New York: Pedigree Books, 1993. (C) (A) (P)

*Between Form and Freedom: A Practical Guide to the Teenage Years*. Betty Staley. United Kingdom: Hawthorn Press, 1988. (A) (P)

*Black Children: Social, Educational, and Parental Environments*. Harriette Pipes McAdoo and John Lewis McAdoo. Beverly Hills, CA: Sage Publications, 1985. (C) (A) (P)

*Black Children: Their Roots, Culture, and Learning Styles*. Janice E. Hale-Benson. Baltimore, MD: The Johns Hopkins University Press, 1982. (C) (A)

*Changing Life Patterns: Adult Development in Spiritual Direction*. Elizabeth Liebert, SNJM. Mahwah, NJ: Paulist Press, 1992. (A)

*Child Behavior*. Frances L. Ilg, M.D., Louise Bates Ames, Ph.D., and Sidney M. Baker, M.D. New York: Harper & Row Publishers, 1981. (C) (P)

---

*A letter designation has been added after each book to indicate:*
*(C) Books about children's development*
*(A) Books about adolescent development*
*(P) Books of interest to parents*
*All books are appropriate for teachers*

---

*Childhood: A Multicultural View*. Melvin Konner. Boston, MA: Little, Brown & Co., 1991. (C) (A) (P)

*Curriculum and Evaluation Standards for School Mathematics*. Prepared by the working groups of the Commission on Standards for School Mathematics of the National Council of Teachers of Mathematics. Reston, VA: The National Council of Teachers of Mathematics, Inc., 1989. (C) (A)

*Dancing Through Walls: Integrated Studies in the Middle Grades*. Chris Stevenson & Judy Carr. New York: Teachers College Press, 1992. (A)

*Development in Early Childhood*. David Elkind. Elementary School Guidance and Counseling, V26 No. 1, pp. 12-21, October 1991. (C) (A)

*The Development of Children*. M. Cole. New York: Scientific American Books, 1989. (C) (A)

*The Diary of Latoya Hunter: My First Year in Junior High*. Latoya Hunter. New York: Crown, 1992. (A) (P)

*First Grade Takes a Test*. Miriam Cohen. New York: Dell Publishing Co., 1980. (C) (P)

"Holistic Education Review". Volume 8, Number 1. Spring 1995. Holistic Education Press, Brandon, VT. (A) (P)

*How to Discipline Your Six to Twelve Year Old . . . Without Losing Your Mind*. Jerry L. Wyckoff, Ph.D. and Barbara C. Unell. New York: Doubleday, 1991. (C) (P)

*How to Talk So Kids Will Learn: At Home and in School*. Adele Faber, Elaine Mazlish. New York: Simon & Schuster, 1995. (C) (A) (P)

*How to Talk So Kids Will Listen and Listen So Kids Will Talk.* Adele Faber, Elaine Mazlish. New York: Avon Books, 1980. (C) (A) (P)

*Identity: Youth and Crisis.* Erik H. Erikson. New York: W.W. Norton & Company, Inc., 1968. (Out of Print) (A)

*In a Different Voice.* Carol Gilligan. Cambridge, MA: Harvard University Press, 1982. (A) (P)

*in my room: teenagers in their bedrooms.* Adrienne Salinger. San Francisco, CA: Chronicle Books, 1995. (A) (P)

*The Magic Years.* Selma H. Fraiberg. New York: Charles Scribner & Sons, 1959. (C) (P)

*Meaning-Making: Therapeutic Processes in Adult Development.* Mary Baird Carlsen. New York: W.W. Norton & Company, Inc., 1988. (A)

*Positive Discipline.* Jane Nelsen. New York: Ballantine Books, (1996). (C) (A) (P)

*The Quality School.* William Glasser, M.D. New York: Harper Collins Publishers, 1990. (C)

*Raising Black Children.* James P. Comer and Alvin F. Poussaint, M.D. New York: Plume, 1992. (C) (A) (P)

---

*A letter designation has been added after each book to indicate:*
*(C) Books about children's development*
*(A) Books about adolescent development*
*(P) Books of interest to parents*
*All books are appropriate for teachers*

---

*Reaching Potentials: Appropriate Curriculum and Assessment for Young Children.* Sue Bredekamp and Teresa Rosegrant. Washington, DC: National Association for the Education of Young Children, 1992. (C)

*Scoring Notes: The Developmental Examination.* Frances Ilg. New Haven, CT: Gesell Institute, 1965. (C)

*The Self Esteem Teacher.* Robert Brooks, Ph.D. Circle Pines, MN: American Guidance Service, 1991. (C) (A)

*Teacher.* Sylvia Ashton-Warner. New York: Bantam, 1971. (C) (A)

*Teaching Children to Care: Management in the Responsive Classroom.* Ruth Sidney Charney. Greenfield, MA: Northeast Foundation for Children, 1992. (C)

*Teaching Ten to Fourteen Year Olds.* Chris Stevenson. White Plains, NY: Longman Publishing Group, 1992. (A)

*Theories of Development: Concepts and Applications.* William C. Crain. Englewood Cliffs, NJ: Prentice-Hall Inc., 1980. (C) (A)

*Touchpoints: Your Child's Emotional and Behavioral Development.* T. Berry Brazelton. Reading, MA: Addison Wesley Publishing Co., 1992. (C) (P)

*Your Child's Growing Mind.* Jane M. Healy, Ph.D. New York: Doubleday, 1987. (C) (P)

*Your Ten to Fourteen Year Old.* Louise Bates Ames, Ph.D., Frances L. Ilg, M.D., and Sidney Baker, M.D. New York: Delacorte Press, 1988. (A) (P)

# Resources for Reading and Writing

*The Art of Teaching Writing*. Lucy Calkins. Portsmouth, NH: Heinemann Educational Books, Inc., 1989. (C) (A)

*The Beginnings of Writing: A practical guide to a young child's discovery of writing through the scribbling, spelling and composing stages*. Charles A. Temple, Ruth G. Nathan and Nancy A. Burris. Boston, MA: Allyn and Bacon, Inc., 1982. (C)

*In the Middle: Writing, Reading and Learning With Adolescents*. Nancy Atwell. Portsmouth, NH: Boynton/Cook Publishers, 1987. (A)

*Independence in Reading*. Don Holdaway. Portsmouth, NH: Heinemann Educational Books, Inc., 1980. (C)

*Invitations: Changing as Teachers and Learners*. Regie Routman. Portsmouth, NH: Heinemann Educational Books, Inc., 1991. (C) (A)

---

*A letter designation has been added after each book to indicate:*
*(C) Books about children's development*
*(A) Books about adolescent development*
*(P) Books of interest to parents*
*All books are appropriate for teachers*

---

# Resource Bibliography for Themes

*Becoming Whole Through Games: A Parent/Teacher Guide and Skill Checklist to 100 Games.* Gwen Bailey Moore, Ph.D. and Todd Serby. Atlanta, GA: TEE GEE Publishing Company, 1988. (C) (A) (P)

*Doing What Scientists Do: Children Learn to Investigate Their World.* Ellen Doris. Portsmouth, NH: Heinemann Educational Books, Inc., 1991. (C)

*I Learn From Children.* Caroline Pratt. New York: Harper & Row, 1970.(Out of Print) (C) (P)

*Learning and Loving It: Theme Studies in the Classroom.* Ruth Gamberg, Winniefred Kwak, Meredith Hutchings, Judy Altheim with Gail Edwards. Portsmouth, NH: Heinemann Educational Books, Inc., 1988. (C)

*Linking Through Diversity: Practical Classroom Methods for Experiencing and Understanding Our Cultures.* Edited by Walter Enloe and Ken Simon. Tucson, AZ: Zephyr Press, 1993. (C) (P)

*Science for All Americans: Scientific Literacy; What Is It ? Why America Needs It. How We Can Achieve It.* F. James Rutherford and Andrew Ahlgren. New York: Oxford University Press, Inc., 1989. (C) (A)

*Young Geographers.* Lucy Sprague Mitchell. New York: Bank Street College of Education, 1991. (C) (A)

# Resource Bibliography for Math

*About Teaching Mathematics: A K–8 Resource.* Marilyn Burns. Sausalito, CA: Math Solutions Publications, 1992. (C) (A)

*Curriculum Evaluation Standards for School Mathematics.* Prepared by the Working Groups of the Commission on Standards for School Mathematics of the National Council of Teachers of Mathematics. Reston, VA: National Council of Teachers of Mathematics, 1989. (C) (A)

*Family Math.* Jean Kerr Stenmark, Virginia Thompson and Ruth Cossey. Berkeley, CA: Regents, University of California, 1986. (C) (P)

*Mathematics Their Way.* Mary Baratta-Lorton. Reading, MA: Addison-Wesley, 1976. (C)

*Young Children Continue to Reinvent Arithmetic-Second Grade.* Constance Kamii. New York, NY: Teachers College Press, 1989. (C)

*Young Children Reinvent Arithmetic.* Constance Kamii. New York: Teachers College Press, 1985. (C)

---

*A letter designation has been added after each book to indicate:*
*(C) Books about children's development*
*(A) Books about adolescent development*
*(P) Books of interest to parents*
*All books are appropriate for teachers*

---

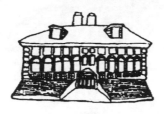

NORTHEAST FOUNDATION FOR CHILDREN

◆

*Resources for Teachers*

Since 1985, Northeast Foundation for Children
has published books on education for those
who believe in the importance of developmentally
appropriate practices and a strong social curriculum
in our schools. In addition to its publishing activities,
Northeast Foundation for Children offers educational
workshops and consulting services and operates
Greenfield Center School, a K-8 school in
Greenfield, Massachusetts.

Additionally, NEFC publishes a newsletter,
*The Responsive Classroom: A Newsletter for Teachers*,
which is mailed three times each year to
educators nationwide. Subscriptions are free.
Please call or write to be added to the mailing list.

## Now Available

*A Notebook for Teachers: Making Changes in the Elementary Curriculum*
by NORTHEAST FOUNDATION FOR CHILDREN STAFF

This timeless resource can help teachers integrate developmentally appropriate teaching techniques into the classroom. *A Notebook for Teachers* includes details on the behavior characteristics of 5, 6 and 7 year olds, as well as classroom implications. This 78-page guide includes over 150 charts, examples, photographs and illustrations.

*Places to Start: Implementing the Developmental Classroom*
Written, Photographed & Presented by MARLYNN K. CLAYTON

This 90-minute classic in the field of developmentally appropriate practices provides a wealth of practical, effective ideas that have been classroom tested over many years. These ideas work to create an active, productive, learning and caring classroom community. From NEFC's acclaimed workshop slideshow, includes 25-page viewing guide.

*Teaching Children to Care: Management in the Responsive Classroom*
by RUTH S. CHARNEY

Speaking to the heart of every classroom teacher, this 314-page book offers a proven, practical approach that helps reduce the exhausting and often overwhelming classroom management problems confronting today's K-8th grade teachers. *Teaching Children to Care* presents theory, practical guidelines, and real-life examples which show how to create classrooms where caring is practiced.

*Yardsticks: Children in the Classroom, Ages 4–14*
by CHIP WOOD

This user-friendly guidebook helps teachers and parents to better understand children by offering clear and concise descriptions of developmental characteristics of each age. Each description is followed by charts with developmental "yardsticks" in the areas of physical, social, language, and cognitive growth. Also included in this 228-page book are curriculum guidelines and a list of favorite books for different ages.

*On Their Side: Helping Children Take Charge of Their Learning*
by BOB STRACHOTA

Written in a personal voice, full of warmth, humor and honesty, the author shares his many effective strategies for helping to create classrooms where children really care about and take responsibility for their learning and behavior. In just 160 pages, Bob Strachota shows how to ally with children, how to ask questions which engage children in real learning, and how to share power with students while also enforcing high standards. Powerful reading for new and experienced teachers alike.

(available April 1997)
*Habits of Goodness: Case Studies in the Social Curriculum*
by RUTH S. CHARNEY

Six experienced public school teachers present case studies in how they think about and work to resolve problems in their classrooms. Ruth Charney, best-selling author of *Teaching Children to Care*, presents commentary on each case, explores classroom management practices, reflects upon the process of problem solving in teachers' professional development, and highlights universal themes which emerge from these case studies.

## For Ordering Information

Publishing Division
NEFC
71 Montague City Rd.
Greenfield, MA 01301

(800) 360-6332 (phone)
(413) 772-2097 (fax)
nefc@crocker.com (email)